❖ ANCIENT WORLD LEADERS ❖

XERXES

◆ ◆ ◆

❖ ANCIENT WORLD LEADERS ❖

XERXES

DENNIS ABRAMS

CHELSEA HOUSE
PUBLISHERS
An imprint of Infobase Publishing

Frontis: *Engraved profile of Xerxes, King of Persia.*

Chelsea House
An imprint of Infobase Publishing
132 West 31st Street
New York, NY 10001

Library of Congress Cataloging-in-Publication Data

Abrams, Dennis, 1960–
  Xerxes / Dennis Abrams.
    p. cm. — (Ancient world leaders)
  Includes bibliographical references and index.
  ISBN-13: 978-0-7910-9602-4 (hardcover)
  1. Xerxes I, King of Persia, 519–465 or 4 B.C. 2. Achaemenid dynasty, 559–330 B.C. 3. Iran—Kings and rulers—Biography. I. Title.
  DS283.A19 2008
  935'.05092—dc22   2007050078

Chelsea House books are available at special discounts when purchased in bulk quantities for businesses, associations, institutions, or sales promotions. Please call our Special Sales Department in New York at (212) 967-8800 or (800) 322-8755.

You can find Chelsea House on the World Wide Web at http://www.chelseahouse.com

Text design by Lina Farinella
Cover design by Jooyoung An

Printed in the United States of America

Bang NMSG 10 9 8 7 6 5 4 3 2 1

This book is printed on acid-free paper.

All links and Web addresses were checked and verified to be correct at the time of publication. Because of the dynamic nature of the Web, some addresses and links may have changed since publication and may no longer be valid.

❖ CONTENTS ❖

Arthur M. Schlesinger, Jr.
On Leadership

L eadership, it may be said, is really what makes the world go round. Love no doubt smoothes the passage; but love is a private transaction between consenting adults. Leadership is a public transaction with history. The idea of leadership affirms the capacity of individuals to move, inspire, and mobilize masses of people so that they act together in pursuit of an end. Sometimes leadership serves good purposes, sometimes bad; but whether the end is benign or evil, great leaders are those men and women who leave their personal stamp on history.

Now, the very concept of leadership implies the proposition that individuals can make a difference. This proposition has never been universally accepted. From classical times to the present day, eminent thinkers have regarded individuals as no more than the agents and pawns of larger forces, whether the gods and goddesses of the ancient world or, in the modern era, race, class, nation, the dialectic, the will of the people, the spirit of the times, history itself. Against such forces, the individual dwindles into insignificance.

So contends the thesis of historical determinism. Tolstoy's great novel *War and Peace* offers a famous statement of the case. Why, Tolstoy asked, did millions of men in the Napoleonic Wars, denying their human feelings and their common sense, move back and forth across Europe slaughtering their fellows? "The war," Tolstoy answered, "was bound to happen simply because it was bound to happen." All prior history determined it. As for leaders, they, Tolstoy said, "are but the labels that serve to give a name to an end and, like labels, they have the least possible connection with the event." The greater the leader, "the more conspicuous the inevitability and the predestination of every act he commits." The leader, said Tolstoy, is "the slave of history."

Determinism takes many forms. Marxism is the determinism of class. Nazism the determinism of race. But the idea of men and women as the slaves of history runs athwart the deepest human instincts. Rigid determinism abolishes the idea of human freedom—the assumption of free choice that underlies every move we make, every word we speak, every thought we think. It abolishes the idea of human responsibility, since it is manifestly unfair to reward or punish people for actions that are by definition beyond their control. No one can live consistently by any deterministic creed. The Marxist states prove this themselves by their extreme susceptibility to the cult of leadership.

More than that, history refutes the idea that individuals make no difference. In December 1931 a British politician crossing Fifth Avenue in New York City between 76th and 77th Streets around 10:30 p.m. looked in the wrong direction and was knocked down by an automobile— a moment, he later recalled, of a man aghast, a world aglare: "I do not understand why I was not broken like an eggshell or squashed like a gooseberry." Fourteen months later an American politician, sitting in an open car in Miami, Florida, was fired on by an assassin; the man beside him was hit. Those who believe that individuals make no difference to history might well ponder whether the next two decades would have been the same had Mario Constasino's car killed Winston Churchill in 1931 and Giuseppe Zangara's bullet killed Franklin Roosevelt in 1933. Suppose, in addition, that Lenin had died of typhus in Siberia in 1895 and that Hitler had been killed on the western front in 1916. What would the 20th century have looked like now?

For better or for worse, individuals do make a difference. "The notion that a people can run itself and its affairs anonymously," wrote the philosopher William James, "is now well known to be the silliest of absurdities. Mankind does nothing save through initiatives on the part of inventors, great or small, and imitation by the rest of us—these are the sole factors in human progress. Individuals of genius show the way, and set the patterns, which common people then adopt and follow."

Leadership, James suggests, means leadership in thought as well as in action. In the long run, leaders in thought may well make the greater difference to the world. "The ideas of economists and political philosophers, both when they are right and when they are wrong," wrote John Maynard Keynes, "are more powerful than is commonly understood. Indeed the world is ruled by little else. Practical men, who believe themselves to be quite exempt from any intellectual influences, are usually the slaves of some defunct economist. . . . The power of vested interests is vastly exaggerated compared with the gradual encroachment of ideas."

But, as Woodrow Wilson once said, "Those only are leaders of men, in the general eye, who lead in action. . . . It is at their hands that new thought gets its translation into the crude language of deeds." Leaders in thought often invent in solitude and obscurity, leaving to later generations the tasks of imitation. Leaders in action—the leaders portrayed in this series—have to be effective in their own time.

And they cannot be effective by themselves. They must act in response to the rhythms of their age. Their genius must be adapted, in a phrase from William James, "to the receptivities of the moment." Leaders are useless without followers. "There goes the mob," said the French politician, hearing a clamor in the streets. "I am their leader. I must follow them." Great leaders turn the inchoate emotions of the mob to purposes of their own. They seize on the opportunities of their time, the hopes, fears, frustrations, crises, potentialities. They succeed when events have prepared the way for them, when the community is awaiting to be aroused, when they can provide the clarifying and organizing ideas. Leadership completes the circuit between the individual and the mass and thereby alters history.

It may alter history for better or for worse. Leaders have been responsible for the most extravagant follies and most monstrous crimes that have beset suffering humanity. They have also been vital in such gains as humanity has made in individual freedom, religious and racial tolerance, social justice, and respect for human rights.

There is no sure way to tell in advance who is going to lead for good and who for evil. But a glance at the gallery of men and women in ANCIENT WORLD LEADERS suggests some useful tests.

One test is this: Do leaders lead by force or by persuasion? By command or by consent? Through most of history leadership was exercised by the divine right of authority. The duty of followers was to defer and to obey. "Theirs not to reason why/ Theirs but to do and die." On occasion, as with the so-called enlightened despots of the 18th century in Europe, absolutist leadership was animated by humane purposes. More often, absolutism nourished the passion for domination, land, gold, and conquest and resulted in tyranny.

The great revolution of modern times has been the revolution of equality. "Perhaps no form of government," wrote the British historian James Bryce in his study of the United States, *The American Commonwealth*, "needs great leaders so much as democracy." The idea that all people should be equal in their legal condition has undermined the old structure of authority, hierarchy, and deference. The revolution of equality has had two contrary effects on the nature of leadership. For equality, as Alexis de Tocqueville pointed out in his great study *Democracy in America*, might mean equality in servitude as well as equality in freedom.

"I know of only two methods of establishing equality in the political world," Tocqueville wrote. "Rights must be given to every citizen, or none at all to anyone . . . save one, who is the master of all." There was no middle ground "between the sovereignty of all and the absolute power of one man." In his astonishing prediction of 20th-century totalitarian dictatorship, Tocqueville explained how the revolution of equality could lead to the *Führerprinzip* and more terrible absolutism than the world had ever known.

But when rights are given to every citizen and the sovereignty of all is established, the problem of leadership takes a new form, becomes more exacting than ever before. It is easy to issue commands and enforce them by the rope and the stake, the concentration camp and the *gulag*. It is much harder to use argument and achievement to overcome opposition and win consent. The Founding Fathers of the United States understood the difficulty. They believed that history had given them the opportunity to decide, as Alexander Hamilton wrote in the first Federalist Paper, whether men are indeed capable of basing government on "reflection and choice, or whether they are forever destined to depend . . . on accident and force."

Government by reflection and choice called for a new style of leadership and a new quality of followership. It required leaders to be responsive to popular concerns, and it required followers to be active and informed participants in the process. Democracy does not eliminate emotion from politics; sometimes it fosters demagoguery; but it is confident that, as the greatest of democratic leaders put it, you cannot fool all of the people all of the time. It measures leadership by results and retires those who overreach or falter or fail.

It is true that in the long run despots are measured by results too. But they can postpone the day of judgment, sometimes indefinitely, and in the meantime they can do infinite harm. It is also true that democracy is no guarantee of virtue and intelligence in government, for the voice of the people is not necessarily the voice of God. But democracy, by assuring the right of opposition, offers built-in resistance to the evils inherent in absolutism. As the theologian Reinhold Niebuhr summed it up, "Man's capacity for justice makes democracy possible, but man's inclination to justice makes democracy necessary."

A second test for leadership is the end for which power is sought. When leaders have as their goal the supremacy of a master race or the promotion of totalitarian revolution or the acquisition and exploitation of colonies or the protection of greed and privilege or the preservation of personal power, it is likely that their leadership will do little to advance the cause of humanity. When their goal is the abolition of slavery, the liberation of women, the enlargement of opportunity for the poor and powerless, the extension of equal rights to racial minorities, the defense of the freedoms of expression and opposition, it is likely that their leadership will increase the sum of human liberty and welfare.

Leaders have done great harm to the world. They have also conferred great benefits. You will find both sorts in this series. Even "good" leaders must be regarded with a certain wariness. Leaders are not demigods; they put on their trousers one leg after another just like ordinary mortals. No leader is infallible, and every leader needs to be reminded of this at regular intervals. Irreverence irritates leaders but is their salvation. Unquestioning submission corrupts leaders and demeans followers. Making a cult of a leader is always a mistake. Fortunately, hero worship generates its own antidote. "Every hero," said Emerson, "becomes a bore at last."

The single benefit the great leaders confer is to embolden the rest of us to live according to our own best selves, to be active, insistent, and resolute in affirming our own sense of things. For great leaders attest to the reality of human freedom against the supposed inevitabilities of history. And they attest to the wisdom and power that may lie within the most unlikely of us, which is why Abraham Lincoln remains the supreme example of great leadership. A great leader, said Emerson, exhibits new possibilities to all humanity. "We feed on genius. . . . Great men exist that there may be greater men."

Great leaders, in short, justify themselves by emancipating and empowering their followers. So humanity struggles to master its destiny, remembering with Alexis de Tocqueville: "It is true that around every man a fatal circle is traced beyond which he cannot pass; but within the wide verge of that circle he is powerful and free; as it is with man, so with communities." ◆

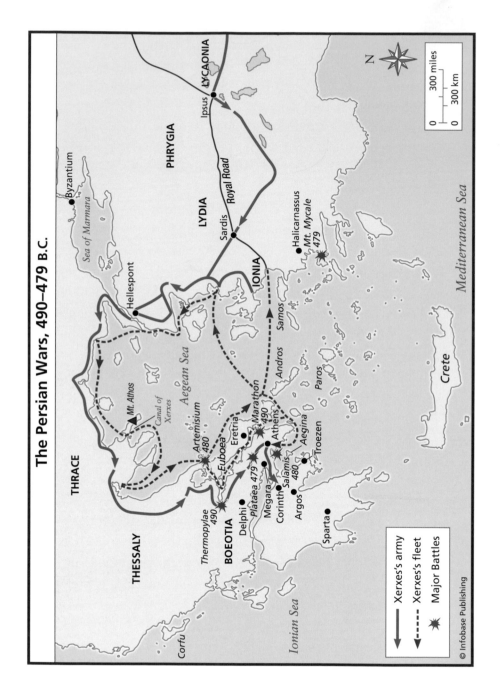

The Persian Wars, 490–479 B.C.

© Infobase Publishing

Xerxes in Ancient History

WHEN WRITING THE BIOGRAPHY OF ANYONE WHO LIVED IN THE TIME THAT we call "ancient history," the biographer runs into a problem. Simply stated, with the occasional exception, there is just not that much that can be known with great certainty about the person's life.

Here, for example, is what is known about Xerxes. He was probably born in the year 519 B.C. We know that his mother's name was Atossa and that his father was Darius, King of Persia. We know that when Darius died in 486 B.C., Xerxes ascended to the throne.

At the beginning of his reign, Xerxes crushed a revolt against his rule in Egypt. He also put down two revolts in Babylon. After consolidating his power in Egypt and Babylonia, he turned his attention to Greece. After winning the Battle of Thermopylae in 480 B.C., his navy lost at the Battle of Salamis. Xerxes was forced to return to Persia, where he reigned as king until the year 465 B.C., when he was murdered by his vizier (a high-ranking political and religious advisor) Artabanos.

That, in a nutshell, is what we know about Xerxes the person. We don't know with certainty what he looked like; our only knowledge is based on stone carvings found in his palace at Persepolis. We don't know what he sounded like. We don't know with any certainty his motivations concerning why he did what he did. We have no quotes taken from the moment he said something; instead, we are forced to rely on the recollections of others, written down years after the fact.

Although we may not know a lot about Xerxes the man, we do know a great deal about what he did during his life. Part of what we know comes from carved reliefs found among the ruins of the Persian (now Iranian) city of Persepolis. We also know about Xerxes and his times from books that were written years after his death. The primary book, the main source of most of our information about Xerxes, is called *The Histories*. Its author was Herodotus, who has been called "the Father of History."

HERODOTUS

Herodotus of Halicarnassus was a Greek historian of the fifth century B.C. He wrote a history of the Persian invasion of Greece, led by Xerxes in the early fifth century B.C., known simply as *The Histories* of Herodotus. This work was quickly recognized as a new form of literature.

Before Herodotus, there had been chronicles and epics, such as Homer's *Iliad*, that had helped to preserve some knowledge of the past. Herodotus was, however, the first writer who not only recorded the past but also treated it as a research project of facts that could yield knowledge of human behavior.

The Greek historian Herodotus's most famous work, *The Histories*, documented wars, geography, and culture from Persia, Egypt, and Sparta. Herodotus conducted interviews with people who had seen and heard what he did not, a method that was new in recordkeeping at the time.

He made his intentions clear in the first paragraph of his work:

> These are the researches of Herodotus of Halicarnassus, which he publishes, in the hope of thereby preserving from decay the remembrance of what men have done, and of preventing the great and wonderful actions of the Greeks and the Barbarians from losing their due meed [reward] of glory, and withal to put on record what were their grounds of feuds.

His great work was published sometime between 430 and 424 B.C. The histories were later divided by editors into nine books or chapters, each named after one of the nine Greek Muses. The first six books deal with the growth of the Persian Empire. They begin with an account of the first Asian monarch to conquer Greek city-states and exact tribute (demand payments honoring the monarch): Croesus of Lydia. Croesus lost his kingdom to Cyrus, who was the founder of the Persian Empire.

The first six books end with the defeat of the Persians at the Battle of Marathon in the year 490 B.C., which was the first setback to their goal of expanding their empire. The last three books of *The Histories* describe Xerxes' attempt 10 years later to avenge the Persian defeat at Marathon by conquering Greece and making it a part of the Persian Empire. *The Histories* ends in 479 B.C., the year the Persian invaders were destroyed at the Battle of Plataea, and the boundary of the Persian Empire receded to the coastline of Asia Minor.

Where did Herodotus get the information necessary to write his histories? How did he do his research? He was not, after all, an eyewitness to any of the events that he wrote about. He could not go to the library to do his research, or read other books. Instead, he traveled and relied on conversations with those who had been witnesses. He also interviewed the grandsons of those who participated in the events described, one of whom may have been the exiled grandson of the former governor of Babylon, Zopyrus.

This method of research raises a very important question: Just how accurate and reliable was Herodotus? There were, after all, no documents to back up the claims of the witnesses, no newspaper accounts of the events. Herodotus himself, on many occasions, is uncertain of the truth of the event or unimpressed by the "facts" that are presented to him. In those cases, he reports several of the more prominent accounts of a given subject or process and then gives his opinion as to which he believes is the most likely to have occurred.

Even still, ever since the books were written, many have questioned his accuracy. In fact, some have called him not "the Father of History" but "the Father of Lies." Yet, although modern scholars have called into question whether he actually

Muses

The nine muses were goddesses that poets, artists, philosophers, and intellectuals appealed to and depended on for the ability to create their works. (In his epic poem *The Aeneid*, the Roman poet Virgil implored "O Muse! the causes and the crimes relate; What goddess was provok'd, and whence her hate. . . ."

The muses and their names probably originated with the Greek poet Hesiod. They were Calliope (epic poetry), Clio (history), Euterpe (flute playing), Terpsichore (lyric poetry and dancing), Erato (lyric poetry), Melpomene (tragedy), Thalia (comedy), Polyhymnia (hymns and pantomime), and Urania (astronomy). These are the classic nine muses, but their names, roles, and number fluctuated.

traveled as much as he said he did and whether he may have fabricated some of his sources, recent archaeological discoveries have tended to verify his assertions.

Another problem inherent in using Herodotus as the primary source for our knowledge of the Greek and Persian wars is that Herodotus himself was Greek. (There are no surviving Persian documents that discuss Xerxes' expedition.) Thus, inevitably, his history—despite his best efforts—is written in favor of the Greeks. This generally tends to be the case, however, since history is written by the winners. (For example, imagine two history textbooks, one American, one English, each written 50 years after the American Revolutionary War. How do you think the American version of the Revolutionary War would differ from the English version? What the American book would see as the bravery and courage of the Founding Fathers the British text would see as treacherous rebels fighting the legitimate English colonial government.)

Note, for example, that in the first paragraph of *The Histories*, cited earlier, Herodotus refers to the Persians as "Barbarians." He saw the Persians from the point of view of the people who won the war. He saw it as a victory for the civilized Greeks over what he viewed as the uneducated, uncivilized Persians.

Of course, it's not as simple as that. It never is. Whereas the Greeks saw the Persians as barbarian invaders, as "outsiders," the Persians saw the Greeks as rebels who refused to acknowledge the strength and prestige of the Persian Empire. After all, at that time the Persian Empire was at its peak, stretching from what is today the country of India to the Balkans, from Central Asia to Egypt. At 7.5 million square kilometers, the empire was, in terms of land, the largest empire of classical antiquity.

The Persians were also a people of religion, ones who designed and built tremendous cities. Their empire was the first in Middle East history to unite the region under one political structure. To the Persians, then, Greece would have seemed like a wild frontier, occupied by a bunch of coarse shepherds.

Three years after the Battle of Marathon, Herodotus documented the conflict. Included in Herodotus's account was the powerful speech given by Miltiades, the Greek general who swayed his peers into commanding a full-force attack on the Persian army.

In addition, the Greeks had caused the Persians a great deal of political trouble over the years. At one time, the Athenians had pleaded with Persia for help and protection from other hostile Greek tribes, but they withdrew their pleas once the danger had passed. More recently, the Greeks on the mainland had supported Greek colonies under Persian rule that had attempted to rebel. This was a direct threat to the empire itself and a slap in the face of Persian authority and rule. It could not be allowed to occur without a military response.

The story of Xerxes, then, is more than just the story of a man who was king. It is the story of the Persian Empire and the rapidly evolving Greek city-states. It is the story of two civilizations, Asian and European, on a collision course. Through the life of Xerxes, the great autocratic king, we see the rise of Greek civilization and the foundation of our own Western cultural heritage.

The Persian Empire

THE ACHAEMENID EMPIRE (559 B.C.–338 B.C.) WAS THE FIRST OF THE PERSIAN Empires to rule over large portions of what is today the country of Iran. Until the twentieth century, the country was known as Persia. On March 21, 1935, the ruler of the country, Reza Shah Pahlavi, issued a decree asking foreign delegates to use the term *Iran* in formal correspondence. His reasoning was that *Persia* was a term only foreigners used for the country; it was called "Iran" by its inhabitants in their native tongue, Persian. Opponents objected to the name change, claiming that it brought cultural damage to the country and separated Iran from its past history. Today, the nation is officially called the Islamic Republic of Iran.

Whether called Persia or Iran, the area has been inhabited by humans since prehistoric times. The written history of Persia

begins in approximately 3200 B.C. with the Proto-Elamite civilization, followed by the Elamites. The arrival of the Aryans
(Indo-Iranians) and the establishment of the Median Dynasty
(728 B.C.–550 B.C.) culminated in the first Persian Empire.

The Medes are credited with the foundation of Persia as a
state and empire. Their empire was the largest of its day until
Cyrus II, known as Cyrus the Great, established a unified empire
of the Medes and Persians that led to the Achaemenian Empire,
founded by Cyrus.

The Achaemenid Empire eventually incorporated the following territories into its control: in the east, modern Afghani-
stan and portions of Pakistan; in the north and west, all of
Turkey (Anatolia), the upper Balkans peninsula (Thrace), and
most of the Black Sea coastal regions; in the west and southwest,
the territories of modern Iraq, northern Saudi Arabia, Palestine (Jordan, Israel, and Lebanon), all major population centers
of ancient Egypt, and as far west along the northern coast of
Africa as portions of Libya. At its peak, it was the largest and
most powerful empire in human history until that point.

The name *Achaemenid* derives from Achaemenes, who
Darius I claimed was an ancestor of Cyrus II the Great and the
progenitor of the entire line of Achaemenid rulers. Achaemenes
was succeeded by his son Teispes, who first took the title King
of Ansan after capturing Ansan City from the Elamites. Inscriptions indicate that when Teispes died, two of his sons shared
the crown as Cyrus, King of Ansan, and Ariaramnes (mean-
ing "having the Iranians at peace"), King of Parsua (later called
Parsa, or Persia). They were succeeded by their respective sons,
Cambyses I of Anshan ("the elder") and Arsames ("having a
hero's might") of Iran (Persia).

In the year 559 B.C., Cambyses I the Elder was succeeded
as king of Ansan by his son, Cyrus II the Great. Cyrus also succeeded the still-living Arsames as king of Persia, reuniting the
two realms of the Medes and the Persians. As a result, Cyrus is
considered to be the first king of the Achaemenid Dynasty.

Although both groups were primarily tribesmen, of the two, the Medes were considered the more sophisticated and advanced. In approximately 612 B.C., they had helped to overthrow the oppressive Assyrian Empire and had ruled in splendor from their capital of Ecbatana.

THE REIGN OF CYRUS II, THE GREAT

After consolidating his power over Media and Persia, Cyrus II quickly moved to expand his realm. He began a campaign of conquest against Lydia (what is today Turkey) after their king, Croesus, attacked the Achaemenid Empire's city of Pteria. The Persians called upon the citizens of Ionia, part of the Lydian kingdom, to revolt against Croesus. The offer was refused. Cyrus assembled an army and marched against the Lydians. By 546 B.C., the Lydians had been defeated. According to Herodotus, Cyrus spared the life of Croesus and kept him on as an advisor, though other sources claim that Croesus was murdered.

The occupants of Lydia were Greeks—thus, this conflict was in fact the first contact between the Persians and the Greeks. As A.T. Olmstead describes it in his book *History of the Persian Empire*, "To the Greeks, Persia was simply one more barbarian monarchy, whose trade their merchants might exploit and, to which, if necessary, the nearer city-states might give a nominal allegiance. . . . To the Persians, however, during the next half-century, Greeks on the western boundary would remain only a minor frontier problem."

After his conquest of Asia Minor, Cyrus turned his sights to Babylonia (what is today Iraq). In 539 B.C., toward the end of September, Cyrus's armies attacked the city of Opis. By the middle of October, his armies had entered Babylon itself. Herodotus explains that, to accomplish this military feat, the Persians diverted the Euphrates River into a canal so that the water level dropped "to the height of the middle of a man's thigh." This allowed the Persian army to march directly through the river-bed during the night.

At the end of October, Cyrus entered the city himself and assumed the titles of "king of Babylon, king of Sumer and Akkad, king of the four sides of the world." The Babylonian Empire had itself conquered many kingdoms. In addition to Babylonia, Cyrus incorporated its own subnational entities into his empire, including Syria and Palestine.

Cyrus the Great was now the ruler of most of the Fertile Crescent, his empire stretching from the eastern parts of Turkey to the Persian Gulf. Unlike many conquerors, Cyrus insisted that he was a liberator. He freed many people who had been brought into the Babylonian Empire as prisoners and slaves. Among those he freed were the Hebrews.

The Hebrews had been brought to Babylon in 587 B.C. by King Nebuchadnezzar. Nebuchadnezzar is known for destroying the great temple built by King Solomon sometime around the year 1000 B.C. Now, under Cyrus, the Hebrews were freed and allowed to return home to Palestine.

Indeed, Cyrus is portrayed in the Bible as the liberator of the Jews. As quoted from the Hebrew bible, Ezra 1:1–8, "In the first year of Cyrus, king of Persia, in order to fulfill the word of the Lord spoken by Jeremiah, the Lord inspired King Cyrus of Persia to issue this proclamation throughout his kingdom, both by word of mouth and in writing: 'Thus says Cyrus, king of Persia: All the kingdoms of the earth the Lord, the God of heaven, has given to me, and he has charged me to build him a house in Jerusalem which is in Judah. Whoever, therefore, among you belongs to any part of his people, let him go up, and may his God be with him!'" To the Jews, Cyrus was a man of God, sent to be their liberator.

Indeed, despite a formidable record of world conquest, Cyrus is known as a pioneer leader in human rights. His empire was primarily political and economic: Newly conquered territories were organized into provinces called satrapies that

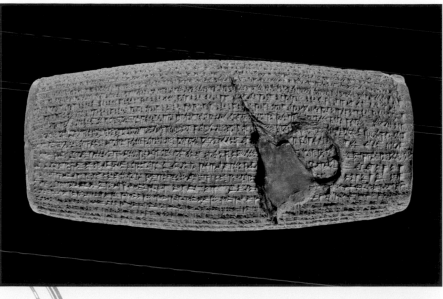

The Cyrus Cylinder *(above)* is an account of Cyrus's conquest of Babylonia. Written in cuneiform, the cylinder praises Cyrus for respecting the Babylonian gods, restoring the city's temples, and releasing foreign subjects from slavery. These actions became symbols of tolerance and respect for other religions, making the Cyrus Cylinder an early declaration of human rights.

were ruled by provincial administrators, vassal kings called sa-traps. The empire demanded only tribute and conscripts for the army from many parts of the realm.

Cyrus allowed the people within his realm to live under the rule of law and to worship whichever gods they chose. Cyrus the Great created the Cyrus Cylinder, which is considered by many to be the first declaration of human rights. He banned slavery throughout the Persian Empire. His ideas on government greatly influenced later human civilizations—for example, his principles of how to rule, which advocated love rather than fear.

His influence is still felt today. On December 10, 2003, in her acceptance of the Nobel Peace Prize, Shirin Ebadi cited Cyrus, saying: "I am an Iranian, a descendant of Cyrus the Great. This emperor proclaimed at the pinnacle of power 2,500 years ago that he 'would not reign over the people if they did not wish it.' He promised not to force any person to change his religion and faith and guaranteed freedom for all. The Charter of Cyrus the Great should be studied in the history of human rights."

DEATH OF CYRUS

At his peak, Cyrus the Great ruled over more land than any ruler before him. Within his empire he ruled over Babylonians, Lydians, former Assyrians, Chaldeans, Bactrians, Phoenicians, and Hebrews. He dreamed of adding Egypt to his empire, but before doing so, he went to the northeastern part of his empire to fight against the Sarmatians and Massagetae. It was here that he was killed in battle—legend has it by Tomyris, the queen of the Massagetae.

His body was returned to his homeland of Parsha. He was buried in the city of Pasargadae, where his tomb remains today. Although the city itself is now in ruins, the burial place of Cyrus the Great has remained largely intact, and the tomb has been partially restored. According to Plutarch in his book, *Life of Alexander,* Cyrus's epitaph read, "O man, whoever you are and wherever you come from, for I know you will come, I am Cyrus who won the Persians their empire. Do not therefore begrudge me this little earth that covers my body."

THE SUCCESSION

Cyrus was succeeded by his son and heir, Cambyses II. Cambyses fulfilled his father's dream by conquering Egypt but died in July 522 B.C., during a revolt led by a sacerdotal clan that had lost its power following Cyrus's conquest of Media.

These priests, who Herodotus called magi, took over the throne with one of their own, named Gautama. Gautama pretended to be Smerdis—younger brother of Cambyses II—who had probably been assassinated three years earlier. Because of

Cambyses's harsh rule and his long absence in Egypt, Herodotus tell us that "the whole people, Perses, Medes and all the other nations" accepted the false ruler, especially because he granted a three-year period without taxes.

According to what is known as the Behistun Inscription, found carved into a limestone cliff on Mount Behistun in Iran, the false Smerdis ruled for seven months before being overthrown in 522 B.C. by a member of a branch of the Achaemenid family, Darius I. One year later, the magi had a second false Smerdis attempt a coup. The coup, although initially successful, failed.

According to Herodotus, the Persian leadership then debated the best form of government for the empire. They decided that a new monarch would be best, and chose Darius I from among the leaders. He was cousin to Cambyses II and Smerdis, and he claimed Ariaramnes as his ancestor.

DARIUS I

Darius I is best remembered for three things: his political consolidation and organization of the Persian Empire, the amazing cities he left behind, and his defeat by the Greeks at the Battle of Marathon.

Darius's method of organizing the vast Persian Empire is thoroughly described by Herodotus (Chapter 3, 89–97). Darius divided the empire into 20 provinces, placing each one under the supervision of a governor or satrap. The satrap position was generally hereditary, passed down from father to son. The satrap worked fairly independently of the central government, with each province having its own laws, traditions, and class structure.

Each province, though, was responsible for paying a gold or silver tribute to the emperor. Many areas, such as Babylonia, fell into severe economic decline as a result of these heavy quotas. Each province also had an independent financial controller and an independent military coordinator as well as the satrap, who was in charge of administration and the law. All three probably reported directly to the king himself. This helped to distribute power within each province more evenly and lower the chance of revolt. Darius also increased the bureaucracy of the empire, employing many scribes to provide records of the administration.

With an empire as vast as the Persian one, rapid communication between the provinces and the king was essential. To inform Darius I, the king of kings, of what was happening in every part of his empire, the Persians developed an ingenious series of couriers, similar to the American pony express. Herodotus described it as follows:

> Nothing mortal travels so fast as these Persian messengers. The entire plan is a Persian invention; and this is the method of it. Along the whole line of road there are men (they say) stationed with horses, in number equal to the number of days which the journey takes, allowing a man and horse to each day; and these men will not be hindered from accomplishing at their best speed the distance which they have to go, either by snow, or heat, or by the darkness of the night. The first rider delivers his dispatch to the second, and the second passes it to the third; and so it is borne from hand to hand along the whole line, like the light in the torch race, which the Greeks celebrate to Hephaestus. The Persians give the riding post in this manner, the name of "Angarum."

It is said that by this method a message could travel from Lydia in Asia Minor, on the western edge of the empire, to Susa in just eight days. The same message, delivered by foot, would take over three months! (You will note, as well, that the U.S. Postal Service takes its motto "Neither rain, nor snow, nor heat,

Darius, seen here with Xerxes standing behind him, was known in the Persian Empire as the ruler who was most like a "shop-keeper." As the first king to enforce and organize tax collection, Darius was able to use this money to build impressive cities like Persepolis, as well as plan for the expansion of his empire.

nor gloom of night stays these couriers from the swift comple-
tion of their appointed rounds" from Herodotus.)

Along with political reorganization, Darius is noted for
instituting other changes as well. Although bronze currency
had been used in China as far back as the eleventh century B.C.,
and the Lydians introduced coins between 643 B.C. and 630 B.C.,
it was Darius who introduced coinage in the form of the *daric*
(gold coin) and the *shekel* (silver coin) within the empire.

He was famed for the ambitious building projects that took place under his rule. The largest laid the groundwork for the new capital of Persepolis. He dug a canal from the Nile to Suez, a forerunner of the modern Suez Canal. (Fragments of a hieroglyphic inscription show that his ships sailed from the Nile through the Red Sea by Saba to Persia.)

Darius also commissioned the extensive road network that was built across the country. The *Persepolis Tablets* describe a

Persepolis

Persepolis, or Parsa, primarily built by Darius I and his son Xerxes I at the height of the Persian Empire, is considered one of the marvels of the ancient world. The city celebrated the king and the office of the monarch. It reflected Darius's (and Xerxes') perception of himself as creator of an empire of disparate peoples whom he united and gave a new and single identity as members of the Persian Empire.

Although the city was looted and burned by Alexander the Great in 331 B.C., the ruins that remain still give a sense of the grandeur that was Persepolis. Excavations on the site revealed that Darius I leveled the rock terrace and began work on the audience hall, the main palace buildings, and the harem (which were completed by Xerxes). Artaxerxes finished what is known as the Hall of a Hundred Pillars and went on to build his own palace on the site.

Around the entire complex was a fortification wall, and a great gate and stairway led up to the terrace. The bas-reliefs of these palaces are considered by many to be among the finest surviving examples of Achaemenid art. These include the audience reliefs (originally flanked by lions attacking bulls) and 23 delegations of tribute bearers of different nations.

"royal road" that ran from Susa to Persepolis and from Sardis to Susa. It was highly organized and included rest stations, guarded garrisons, and roadside inns.

The empire was at peace, and its days of expansion were over, when Darius heard distressing news. The Ionians were in revolt against his empire. Aided by the Athenians, they had burned down the city of Sardis in the province of Lydia. According to Herodotus, upon hearing the news Darius asked, "Who are these Athenians?" He would learn soon enough, as the struggle for power between the Greeks and Persia would determine the future of western civilization.

CHAPTER

3

The Athenians

THE GREECE OF DARIUS'S TIME WAS NOT A NATION AS WE UNDERSTAND it, or even a single geographic entity. The Greek-speaking people lived not only on mainland Greece but also had settled throughout the eastern Mediterranean, colonizing islands in the Aegean Sea and establishing settlements in southern Italy and Sicily and all along the coast of Asia Minor.

They remained a tribal people, organizing themselves into independent communities. The city (*polis*) became the basic unit of Greek government; the cities were originally monarchies. Power lay with a small class of landowners, who formed a warrior aristocracy that fought frequent intercity wars over land.

By the sixth century B.C., several cities emerged as dominant in Greek affairs: Athens, Sparta, Corinth, and Thebes. Each had brought the surrounding rural areas and smaller towns under its control. Athens and Corinth became major maritime and mercantile powers, as well. Athens and Sparta developed a rivalry that would dominate Greek politics for generations.

In Sparta, the landed aristocracy retained their power and gave Sparta a permanent military regime under a dual monarchy. Sparta dominated the other cities of the Peloponnese, with the exceptions of Argus and Achaia.

In Athens, the monarchy was abolished in 683 B.C., and the reforms of Solon established a moderate system of aristocratic government. By the year 500 B.C., Cleisthenes had established the world's first democracy in Athens. The power was held not by a small group of landowners but by an assembly of all the male citizens. This represented the birth of democracy as we know it. It must be remembered, though, that only a small minority of all male inhabitants of Athens were actually citizens—the rest were slaves, freedmen, and non-Athenians.

WAR

In this period of history, the western part of what is now Turkey was dominated by Greeks. (The Turks did not arrive until 1,500 years later.) The cities there, including such great centers as Miletus and Halicarnassus, had come under the rule of the Persian Empire in the mid-sixth century B.C. In 499 B.C., the Greeks there rose up in the Ionian revolt. The citizens of Athens and Eretria, who wanted to help free their fellow Greeks from Persian domination, rushed to their aid.

Darius sent his forces to Ionia to crush the revolt. Afterward, he sent ambassadors to the Greek mainland and demanded that the city-states there show their submission to him by giving offerings of earth and water. Legend has it that when he heard that the Spartans threw the ambassadors down a deep well and left them to die, Darius decided to punish the Greeks.

It is also said that Darius had sworn vengeance against the Athenians when he heard about the burning of Sardis and instructed a servant to remind him three times each day of his vow. It is clear, though, that Darius was unaware of the existence of the Athenians before the attack—so vast was the Persian Empire and so insignificant were the Greek people.

In 492 B.C., Darius sent his son-in-law Marodonius to affirm Persian control in the provinces of Thrace and Macedonia. Darius wanted to make sure that these lands (now southern Bulgaria and northern Greece, respectively) were safely under control before he invaded Greece. The Persian land campaign was a success. Thrace and Macedonia submitted to the Persian army led by Mardonius, and Persian control soon reached to Mount Olympus, on the northern border of Thessaly.

The Persian fleet, on the other hand, suffered a disastrous loss. Most of the navy was lost off the coast of Mount Athos, the easternmost point of the Chalcidice Peninsula, in a terrible storm.

In 490 B.C., Darius sent a naval fleet and army from Asia Minor to the Greek mainland. Darius himself was not among them; he placed his trust in his commanders, Datis and Artaphernes.

After landing on the Aegean island of Naxos, the Persians moved on to Euboea. There, on Darius's orders, his army attacked Eretria, destroying the city and enslaving its citizens. This act backfired on Darius—the brutality of the attack made especially clear to the Athenians how they would be treated by the Persians if they were defeated by them.

Unlike the Persians, the Greeks did not have a system of horse riders to send communications. Instead, they relied on a series of runners to fill the same role. Upon learning of their imminent danger, the Athenians sent a runner named Pheidippides to Sparta to ask for assistance. The Spartans agreed to help, but, being superstitious, said they could not go to war until the Carneian festival ended on the full moon.

Terribly outnumbered at the Battle of Marathon, the Greek generals rallied their troops and managed to defeat the Persians in an unlikely and triumphant victory that is commemorated annually with a modern-day marathon competition.

Because of this, the only Greeks to stand by the Athenians in battle were the Plataeans. The Greeks and the Persians amassed their men on a rocky headland overlooking the plain of Marathon, about 25 miles northeast of Athens. It is estimated that there were 10,000 Athenians and 1,000 Plataeans fighting against an army of somewhere between 20,000 and 60,000 Persians.

The Greek warriors, called *hoplites*, wore light armor and held spears. The Persians, awaiting the attack on the beach, wore leather and carried axes and swords. Led by the Athenian general Miltiades, the Greeks suddenly charged the Persian army on foot. The Greeks fought with a newfound fury, determined to beat the Persians and drive them off the Greek mainland. Herodotus described the moment of attack from the Greek perspective:

> The Athenians, so soon as they were let go, charged the barbarians at a run. Now the distance between the two armies was little short of eight furlongs [a little less than a mile]. The Persians, therefore, when they saw the Greeks coming on at speed, made ready to receive them, although it seemed to them that the Athenians were bereft of their senses, and bent on their own destruction; for they saw a mere handful of men coming on at a run without either horsemen or archers. Such was the opinion of the barbarians; but the Athenians in close array fell upon them, and fought in a manner worthy of being recorded. They were the first of the Greeks, so far as I know, who introduced the custom of charging the enemy at a run, and they were likewise the first who dared to look upon the Persian garb, and to face men clad in that fashion. Until this time the very name of the Persians had been a terror to the Greeks to hear.

When the battle was over, the Greeks had won an overwhelming victory. More than 6,000 Persians were killed, and seven Persian ships had been captured. The Athenians lost fewer than 200 men, the Plateans only 11.

To give thanks to Athena, the patron goddess of the city, Athens began construction of the Parthenon temple on top of the Acropolis, the hill overlooking the city. (The Parthenon was still not complete 10 years later, when the Persians returned.) Legend has it that, after the battle, the Greek messenger Pheidippides ran from the battlefield to Athens, informing the citizens of the great victory before collapsing. It is from this tale, according to legend, that the modern day sport of marathon was born.

Acropolis

The Acropolis of Athens is the best-known *acropolis* (high city, or "Sacred Rock") in Greece. It is a flat-topped rock that rises 512 feet above sea level in the city of Athens, Greece. Although it has been inhabited since the sixth millennium B.C., and the temples were erected as early as the mid-sixth century B.C., most of the major temples were rebuilt under the leadership of Pericles during the Golden Age of Athens (460 B.C.–430 B.C.). Of those temples, the most famous and enduring is the Parthenon.

The Parthenon is a temple for the goddess Athena. It is considered the most famous surviving building of ancient Greece, and it has been praised as the highest achievement of Greek architecture. An enduring symbol of ancient Greece and Athenian democracy, it is rightly regarded as one of the world's great cultural monuments.

The name likely derives from the monumental ivory and gold statue of Athena Parthenos that was housed in the eastern room of the building. The Parthenon replaced an older temple of Athena that had been destroyed by the Persians in 480 B.C. Like most Greek temples, it was also used as a treasury.

In the sixth century A.D., the Parthenon was converted into a Christian church dedicated to the Virgin Mary. Following the Turkish conquest, it was converted into a mosque. In 1687, a Turkish ammunition dump inside the building was ignited by a Venetian cannonball, and the resulting explosion severely damaged both the building and its sculptures. In the nineteenth century A.D., Lord Elgin removed some of the surviving sculptures and took them to England for safekeeping. These sculptures, now known as the Elgin Marbles (or Parthenon Marbles), are on display at the British Museum. There is an ongoing dispute concerning whether the Elgin Marbles should be returned to Greece.

The Parthenon, along with the other buildings on the Acropolis, is one of the most visited archaeological sites in Greece. The Greek Ministry of Culture is currently carrying out a program of restoration and reconstruction.

As a tribute to Athena, the Greeks began to build the Parthenon temple after their victory at Marathon. Located at the Acropolis, the temple was a long-term building project and was still under construction when the Persians attacked again, ten years later.

For Darius, the defeat at Marathon was a major loss and a huge blow to the prestige of the Persian army. Until then, the army had been considered nearly invincible by the people of the Persian Empire. This loss demonstrated to other provinces that resistance against the mighty Persians was indeed possible. The victorious Greeks, on the other hand, were strengthened. As J.F.C. Fuller said in *A Military History of the Western World*, "their victory endowed the Greeks with a faith in their destiny that was to endure for three centuries, during which western culture was born."

A DREAM OF REVENGE

Immediately following the return of the expedition, Darius began preparations for a second, full-scale invasion of Greece. Reviewing the reasons for his loss, Darius came to realize that he had put too much trust in his generals—Datis, in particular. The king decided that, when it came time to attack Greece again, he would have to lead the army himself to restore confidence in both his own leadership and that of his empire.

For the next three years, Darius concentrated on rebuilding his army. Taxes were raised throughout the empire to pay for the expanded military. Egypt, in particular, which already provided much of the grain for the empire, toiled under a particularly heavy tax burden. In the winter of 486, the Egyptians revolted.

Given the vital importance of Egypt to the empire, Darius was forced to turn his attentions away from plans for the Greek invasion and to concentrate instead on putting down the rebellion. Making matters even worse, Darius became seriously ill. He had never completely recovered from his loss at Marathon, and the revolt in Egypt was an additional burden he could not handle.

Darius died in 486 B.C., probably in the month of October. He had ruled the Persian Empire for 36 years. Darius had brought the empire to new heights of power and prestige, but he left behind a rebellion in Egypt and unfinished plans for a new invasion of Greece. It would be up to Darius's son and chosen heir, Xerxes, to complete his father's plans. He was most likely in his early thirties and had lived in his father's shadow his entire life. Would he be up to the task? Was Xerxes ready to become the next king of kings?

4

Young Xerxes

ACCORDING TO HERODOTUS, DARIUS HAD NUMEROUS WIVES. HIS FIRST
wife, whom he married before he became king, was the daughter of the Persian general Gobryas. Upon his ascension to the throne, he took two more wives.

Atossa, who was Xerxes' mother, was the daughter of Cyrus the Great and had been married twice before. Her first marriage was to her own brother, the emperor Cambyses. After his death, she was forced to marry the "false" emperor, Smerdis. When Darius overthrew Smerdis, he married Atossa as well, along with her sister Artystone. He also took other wives: Parmys, a granddaughter of Cyrus; a daughter of Otanes, who had discovered the truth about the false Smerdis; and finally his niece Phratagune.

Obviously, polygamy (having several wives) was an essential part of Persian royal life. In addition to his wives, Darius also had concubines (women who lived in the harem). The Persians felt that the more wives, women, and children the king had reflected favorably on his wealth, power, and prestige.

With numerous wives and concubines to choose from, Darius was the father of many children. With his first wife Gobryas, he had his oldest son, Artabazanes, along with two other children, Ariabignes and a son whose name is not recorded. With Atossa, he had his second oldest son, Xerxes, as well as Achaemenes, Hystaspes, Masistes, and Mandane. With Artystone, he had Arsames, Gobryas, and Artazostre. With Parymas, he had Ariomardus. With Phratagune, he had Abrocomes and Hyperanthes. In addition to these, he fathered numerous other children whose mothers remain unknown.

Xerxes and his brothers and sisters, along with Darius's wives and concubines, lived in Darius's palace at Susa. Xerxes lived in his father's harem, the separate women's quarters in the palace, where he received his education from a private tutor. He learned to read and write the Aryan language, with its 36-character alphabet. He learned about the nations that made up his father's empire and what resources each of them provided. He learned what it would take to run an empire. As the son of a great warrior, he also learned the skills necessary to fight for and serve his father's empire.

Xerxes grew up surrounded by wealth and luxury. The Persian Empire was the richest and largest empire the world had ever seen, and the king's palaces reflected that wealth. Building materials and workmen were imported from all corners of the empire to construct the royal palaces at Susa and Persepolis.

In describing the construction of his palace at Susa, Darius noted:

The cedar timber from there (a mountain by the name Lebanon) was brought, the yaka timber was brought from

Gandara and from Carmania. The gold was brought from Sardis and from Bactria . . . the precious stone lapis-lazuli and carnelian . . . was brought from Sogdiana. The turquoise from Chorasmia, the silver and ebony from Egypt, the ornamentation from Ionia, the ivory from Ethiopia and from Sind and from Arachosia. The stone-cutters who wrought the stone, those were Ionians and Sardians. The goldsmiths were Medes and Egyptians. The men who wrought the wood, those were Sardinians and Egyptians. The men who wrought the baked brick, those were Babylonians. The men who adorned the wall, those were Medes and Egyptians.

This was an imperial art on an unprecedented scale. Materials and artists were drawn from all of the lands ruled by the great kings. Their tastes, styles, and motifs became mixed together in an eclectic art and architecture that symbolized the empire and how the kings thought it should function.

RELIGION

Religion was an essential part of young Xerxes' life. It was during the Achaemenid period that Zoroastrianism reached what is today southwestern Iran. Here it was accepted by the rulers and, through them, became a defining element of Persian culture.

Zoroastrianism is the religion and philosophy ascribed to the prophet Zoroaster (also known as Zarathustra or Zartosht). Mazdaism is the religion that acknowledges the divine authority of Ahuramazda, who was proclaimed by Zoroaster to be the uncreated creator of all (God). According to Zoroastrian creed and articles of faith, the two are virtually synonymous. In a declaration of faith, the adherent states, "I profess myself devotee of Mazda, a follower of Zarathustra."

In the simplest of terms, the believer believes in the god Ahuramazda; he believes that creation is under attack by

The kings who built the great cities of the Persian Empire believed that the architecture and art used in construction should reflect the expanse and diversity of their civilization. Cyrus used symbols of the religion Zoroastrianism, like this one of Ahuramazda, in building motifs throughout Persepolis.

forces of violence and destruction, with Ahuramazda ultimately winning; he believes in active participation in life through good thoughts, words, and deeds; and he believes in the concept of free will, that people have the freedom to decide for themselves whether to perform good thoughts, words, and deeds.

Under the Achaemenid kings, Zoroastrianism reached all parts of the empire. Herodotus wrote, "[The Perses] have no images of the gods, no temples nor altars, and consider the use of them a sign of folly. This comes, I think, from their not believing the gods to have the same nature with men, as the Greeks imagine."

Herodotus claimed that the Persians offered sacrifice to "the sun and moon, to the earth, to fire, to water, and to the winds." The morning ritual, the greeting of the rising sun, was an essential part of everyday life. As Morgan Llywelyn pointed out in his biography *Xerxes*, although there were no temples, the Persians did have altars:

> Their religion centered around altars erected on hilltops, in palaces, and at the center of cities. Around these altars prayers were chanted to the sun—the Undying Fire—until midday. Offerings of flowers and bread were carefully

Xerxes in the Bible

In the biblical Book of Ezra, Xerxes I is mentioned by the Hebrew name of Ahashverosh (Ahasuerus in Greek). During his reign and those of his father, Darius, and his son Artaxerxes, many Samaritans petitioned the Persian king with accusations against the Jews.

Xerxes is also believed to be Ahasuerus the King in the biblical Book of Esther. In this book, Ahasuerus dismissed his queen consort, Vashti, because she refused to obey his command to appear as "queen of his empire" at a feast he was having for his princes. After sending forth a decree to gather the prettiest young virgins from throughout his empire, he chose the Jewish Esther as his queen. The king's minister Haman, an Agagite (a nation that was decreed by God to be destroyed)—feeling insulted by Esther's uncle Mordecai because he would not bow down to him—convinced Ahasuerus to order the destruction of all the Jews in the Persian Empire. Mordecai and Esther convinced the king to reverse his decree, however, and Haman ended up on the gallows. The Jewish festival of Purim celebrates this story.

arranged and livestock sacrificed to the sun—the embodi-
ment of the god known as Ahuramazda—the Wise Lord.

There were other gods of course. Astivihad, god of death, was
always looking over the shoulders of warriors, but the priests
taught that a:

> man who was truthful and pious could face Astivihad with-
> out fear. As for Anaitis, goddess of vegetation and fertility,
> the women as well as the priests conducted sacred rites in
> her honor. Religion was a powerful force in Persia.

CUSTOMS

There was more to Xerxes' life than education and religion. For
example, Herodotus noted that the Persians loved celebrating
birthdays with great feasts, followed by many desserts, a treat
that they reproached the Greeks for not including in their
meals. Herodotus also observed that the Persians were fond of
drinking wine in large quantities and even used it for council.
They discussed important matters when drunk, and the next
day—when sober—would decide whether to act on their decision or set it aside.

Herodotus asserted that when equals met, they kissed on
the lips; that persons of some difference in rank kissed on the
cheek; and that the lowest ranks prostrated themselves on the
ground to the upper ranks.

We also learn from Herodotus that the Persians had a very
high regard for truth. They taught the respect of truth to their
children and hated nothing more than a lie. On the education
of children, we learn from Herodotus that from the age of five
to the age of 20, boys were taught to ride, shoot the bow, and
speak the truth.

It is also interesting to note that, until the age of five, children spent all their time among the women and never met their

father. This way, should they die in infancy, the father would not grieve too much over their loss.

WHO WILL SUCCEED DARIUS?

By the year 490 B.C., Xerxes was a crown prince of Persia. He was a trained military commander who had led several major military expeditions. He had served as viceroy in Babylon, where he had overseen the construction of Darius's palace there. He also served as royal presence at the great palace at Persepolis when Darius was not in attendance.

Xerxes was, in fact, first portrayed in art at Persepolis. On the facing jambs of a gateway are two carved reliefs. The first is of Darius, clad in his robe, sitting on his throne. Behind him stands Xerxes, wearing the same robes and the same long, square-cut beard. Because he is only crown prince, he stands humbly behind his father. Xerxes raises his right hand toward Darius's throne, palm open, in the usual gesture of worship made to Ahuramazda. The reliefs display to all who see them the power of the Persian king and his son.

Xerxes was not necessarily destined to become the next king; others might have had a greater claim to the throne. According to Persian law, Darius—before leading his armies to battle in Egypt—would have to appoint the man who would become the next king. Herodotus wrote:

> Darius, before he obtained the kingdom, had three sons born to him from his former wife, who was a daughter of Gobryas; while, since he began to reign, Atossa, the daughter of Cyrus, had borne him four. Artabazanes was the eldest of the first family, and Xerxes of the second. These two, therefore, being the sons of different mothers, were now at variance. Artabazanes claimed the crown as the eldest of all the children, because it was an established custom for the eldest to have the pre-eminence; while Xerxes, on the other

hand, urged that he had sprung from Atossa, the daughter of Cyrus, and that it was Cyrus who had won the Persians their freedom.

Before Darius had reached his decision, Demaratus, a Spartan, arrived at Susa and heard of the argument between the princes. According to Herodotus, he gave Xerxes the following advice:

> Hereupon, as report says, he went to Xerxes, and advised him, in addition to all that he had urged before, to plead— that at the time when [Xerxes] was born Darius was already king and bore rule over the Persians; but when Artabazanes came into the world, he was a mere private person. It would therefore be neither right nor seemly that the crown should go to another in preference to himself. "For at Sparta," said Demaratus, by way of suggestion, "the law is, that if a king has sons before he comes to the throne, and another son is born to him afterwards, the child so born is heir to his father's kingdom." Xerxes followed this counsel, and Darius, persuaded that he had justice on his side, appointed him his successor. For my own part I believe that, even without this, the crown would have gone to Xerxes, for Atossa was all-powerful.

Atossa was indeed all powerful. Some sources indicate that she was the only one of Darius's wives to be referred to as "Queen." According to Herodotus, it was also by her urging that Darius invaded Greece, leading to the disastrous defeat at Marathon.

The next year, 486 B.C., Darius died at age 64. Xerxes would become the next king. He was probably in his early thirties when he ascended to the throne. The day he was crowned was a holiday throughout the empire. Feasts were held and sacrifices were offered for the success of the new king.

The buildings and columns constructed by the great Persian kings like Xerxes always contained some form of artwork involving mythical creatures, Zoroastrianism, or their own images. Many depictions of these kings were also accompanied by pronouncements of their leadership or achievements.

At Persepolis, Xerxes laid down a clay tablet to inform the world how he became king:

> Says Xerxes the king: My father was Darius. The father of Darius was by name Vishtaspa. The father of Vishtaspa was by name Arshama. Vishtaspa and Arshama were both living when Ahuramazda, by his will, made Darius my father king of the earth. Darius also had other sons, but by the will of Ahuramazda, Darius my father made *me* the greatest after himself. When Darius my father passed away, by the will of Ahuramazda I became king on my father's throne.

Thus, by the will of the god Ahuramazda, Xerxes was now the ruler of the largest empire in the world. He was no longer just a man—it was believed that the voice of the sun spoke directly through him. He would have to prove himself worthy of being king, and he would have to complete the jobs that his father had left unfinished; namely, he needed to bring the Egyptians back firmly under Persian control. Only then could he turn his attention to Athens and the Greeks and punish them for his father's defeat at Marathon.

His first task as king, however, was to complete his father's palace at Susa, where a few columns still remained to be carved. There, near the beginning of his reign, Xerxes prepared an inscription to commemorate and proclaim his new authority:

> A great god is Ahuramazda, who created this earth, who created man, who created peace for man, who made Xerxes king, one king of many, one lord of many.
>
> I am Xerxes, the great king, king of kings, king of lands containing many men, king in this great earth far and wide, son of Darius the king, an Achaemenid, a Persian, son of a

Persian, an Aryan, of Aryan seed. Says Xerxes the king: By the favor of Ahura Mazda, these are the lands of which I am king outside Parsa.

The known world now belonged to Xerxes. Would he be able to finish his father's work and establish his own greatness?

CHAPTER

5

Decisions

WHEN XERXES TOOK THE THRONE, HE HAD SEVERAL IMPORTANT MILITARY decisions to make. Personally, he was not inclined to attack Greece; he felt it was vital for him to amass an army and move against Egypt.

Many of his advisors, however, advised him on the importance of attacking Greece. According to Herodotus, Xerxes' cousin Mardonius told him:

> Master, it is not fitting that they of Athens escape scot-free, after doing the Persians such great injury. Complete the work which thou hast now in hand, and then, when the pride of Egypt is brought low, lead an army against Athens. So shalt

thou thyself have good report among men, and others shall fear hereafter to attack thy country.

Why would Mardonius advise this? Like many advisors, he had his own agenda. Herodotus noted that Mardonius hoped to become satrap of Greece under Xerxes after the conquest was complete.

Other voices also encouraged Xerxes to move against the Greeks. Onomacritus of Athens, an oracle (someone who was thought to be able to foretell the future), informed Xerxes that he was destined to take over Greece. "Twas fated," he told Xerxes, "that a Persian should bridge the Hellespont, and march an army from Asia into Greece."

Xerxes, initially reluctant, began to come around to the point of view of those in favor of attacking Greece. Yet, before he could do so, he would have to put down rebellions within the empire itself.

EGYPT AND BABYLONIA

One year after his father's death, Xerxes led his troops against Egypt. By the beginning of the year 484 B.C., Egypt had been recovered. Once again, the empire received building stone from the quarries of Egypt, and grain was being shipped to Persia.

Xerxes was determined that the Egyptians would never rise in revolt again. Previously under Persian rule, Egypt had held privileged status in the empire. The Persian king, allowing the Egyptians some semblance of freedom, had assumed within Egypt the traditional role of pharaoh and kept the Egyptian traditions intact. Under Xerxes, however, Egypt would be ruled from without—just like any other conquered nation. Once the domination of Egypt was complete, Xerxes left his brother Achaemenes in charge as satrap. The Egyptians were now a subject people.

Babylonia was the next trouble spot for Xerxes. Initially, the Babylonians were happy with Xerxes as king (he had spent much time in Babylon as viceroy). Soon, though, his increased taxes (to rebuild the Persian army) and repressive measures put in place to stop any hint of rebellion roused the anger of the Babylonian people.

In 482 B.C., a Babylonian pretender to the throne assassinated the Persian satrap and took for himself the title of king. Xerxes could not allow this to go unpunished. He sent his brother-in-law Megabyzus, a highly experienced general, to Babylonia to reassert Persian authority.

Just as in Egypt, he took away Babylonia's special position of independence and reestablished Persian domination. Under Xerxes' orders, Megabyzus sacked Babylon. He destroyed building after building and took the wealth of Babylon back to Persia. Whole Babylonian estates were taken from their owners and given to Persian noblemen. As a final insult, the great king ordered the removal of the colossal gold statue of Marduk, the Babylonian god, from Babylon. This statue, the symbol of the legitimacy of the Babylonian monarch, was melted down into gold bars for the Persian treasury.

With Egypt and Babylonia firmly under Persian control, Xerxes could turn his attention to Greece. Although his treatment of the two nations might seem severe by today's standards (or perhaps not), Xerxes lived in different times. A king could not show any sign of weakness that might lead others to attack him. In order to control an empire as vast as his, kindness, he felt, was not a viable policy.

At the same time, Xerxes had his own family to consider. He had married his first wife when he was young; by the time he became king, he had sired numerous children by his many wives and concubines. His favorite son (although not his eldest) was partially named after him: Artaxerxes, which means "justice of Xerxes." Xerxes' own name translates from Persian as "hero among kings."

When Xerxes became king of the Persian Empire, he took away the independence of Egypt and Babylonia and even destroyed a large gold idol of the Babylonian god Marduk *(above)* from the region. This sent a clear message to those who rose against Xerxes that he was the undisputed king and they were his subjects.

Not only was Xerxes a "hero among kings," he also—based on surviving sculptures, at least—looked the part. He was a tall, handsome man, with a strong face and physique. According to American historian Will Durant, "Xerxes was every inch a king—externally; tall and vigorous, he was by royal consent the handsomest man in his empire."

Based on what we know about Persian noblemen in general, he was vain about his good looks as well. Persian noblemen spent a great deal of time enhancing their looks with cosmetics (using eyeliner, in the Egyptian manner) and arranging their hair in layers of elaborate curls, held in place with aromatic oils. Whoever looked at Xerxes would know at a glance that he was a king.

Pyramids of Egypt

From our modern perspective, it is easy to look back at Xerxes and the Persian Empire as "ancient history"—and, of course, it is. But the following bit of information should help put that concept into perspective.

Although there is no historical record of the event, one would think it likely that, when Xerxes led the Persian Army into Egypt in the year 485 B.C. to quell a rebellion, he saw the Great Pyramids of Giza, located outside of Cairo. Xerxes, like every visitor to the site, would have gazed in wonder at the pyramids, dumbstruck by their size and awed by their construction. Yet, consider this: When Xerxes was in Egypt, the pyramids had already been standing for more than 2,000 years—almost as much time as has elapsed between Xerxes and us!

THE DECISION IS MADE

As king, the decision to invade Greece was ultimately his to make. That scattered cluster of independent city-states in no way posed a direct threat to the national security of Persia. Still, Xerxes felt the call to conquer Greece and the Athenians and to avenge his father's defeat. Darius had left the job unfinished; it would be up to his son to complete the task.

There were other considerations, as well. By conquering Greece and expanding the Persian Empire, Xerxes would be able to elevate his name and reputation to that of his illustrious predecessors, Cyrus the Great and Darius. In Xerxes' time, going to war was the way to prove one's greatness.

Before reaching a final decision, Xerxes called a grand council of the "noblest Persians" to learn their opinions and to inform them of his plans. When the council met, Xerxes addressed the nobles:

> Persians, I shall not be the first to bring in among you a new custom—I shall but follow one which has come down to us from our forefathers. Never yet, as our old men assure me, has our race reposed itself, since the time when Cyrus overcame Astyages, and so we Persians wrested the scepter from the Medes. Now in all this God guides us: and we, obeying his guidance, prosper greatly. What need do I have to tell you of the deeds of Cyrus and Cambyses, and my own father Darius, how many nations they conquered, and added to our dominions? Ye know right well what great things they achieved. But for myself, I have not ceased to consider by what means I may rival those who have preceded me in this post of honor, and increase the power of Persia as much as any of them. And truly I have pondered upon this until at last I have found out a way whereby we may at once win glory, and likewise get possession of a land which is as large and as rich as our own—nay, which is even

more varied in the fruits it bears—while at the same time we obtain satisfaction and revenge. For this cause I have now called you together, that I may make known to you what I design to do.

My intent is to throw a bridge over the Hellespont and march an army through Europe against Greece, and that thereby I may obtain vengeance from the Athenians for the wrongs committed by them against the Persians and against my father. Your own eyes saw the preparations of Darius against these men; but death came upon him, and balked his hopes of revenge. In his behalf, therefore, and in behalf of all the Persians, I undertake the war, and pledge myself not to rest until I have taken and burnt Athens, which has dared, unprovoked, to injure me and my father. . . .

Once let us subdue this people, and those neighbors of those who hold the land of Pelops the Phrygian, and we shall extend the Persian territory as far as God's heaven reaches. The sun will then shine on no land beyond our borders; for I will pass through Europe from one end to the other, and with your aid make of all the lands which it contains one country. For thus, if what I hear be true, affairs stand: The nations whereof I have spoken, once swept away, there is no city, no country left in all the world, which will venture so much as to withstand us in arms. By this course then we shall bring all mankind under our yoke, alike those who are guilty and those who are innocent of doing us wrong.

For yourselves, if you wish to please me, do as follows: When I announce the time for the army to meet together, hasten to the muster with a good will, every one of you; and know that to the man who brings with him the most gallant array I will give the gifts which our people consider the most honorable. This then is what ye have to do. But to show that I am not self-willed in this matter, I lay the business before you, and give you full leave to speak your minds upon it openly.

As Xerxes contemplated engaging in war with Greece, he was reminded of his father's failure in the Battle of Marathon. The Greeks' defeat of Darius *(above)* against Greece was an embarrassment to the Persian Empire, and government ministers had no desire to see another abandoned attempt at Greek expansion.

According to Herodotus, Mardonius spoke first, praising the greatness of Xerxes and predicting an easy victory:

> Of a truth, my lord, thou dost surpass, not only all living Persians, but likewise those yet unborn. . . . It were indeed a monstrous thing if, after conquering and enslaving the Sacae, the Indians, the Ethiopians, the Assyrians, and many other mighty nations, not for any wrong that they had done us, but only to increase our empire, we should then allow the Greeks, who have done us such wanton injury, to escape our vengeance. What is it that we fear in them—not surely their numbers?—not the greatness of their wealth? We know the manner of their battle—we know how weak their power is. . . . And I am told these very Greeks are wont to wage wars against one another in the most foolish way, through sheer perversity and doltishness. . . . Who will then dare, O king! to meet thee in arms, when thou comest with all Asia's warriors at they back, and with all her ships? For my part I do not believe the Greek people will be so foolhardy. Grant, however, that I am mistaken herein, and that they are foolish enough to meet us in open fight; in that case they will learn that there are no such soldiers in the whole world as we.

When Mardonius finished his speech, a silence fell among the crowd. Although there were many present who had doubts about the wisdom of invading Greece, no one had the courage to speak out and oppose the king. Finally, Xerxes' uncle Artabanos spoke. He advised Xerxes that the fight against Greece was filled with dangers, and that the Greeks would fight bravely and courageously to defend their homeland. He reminded Xerxes of the defeat that Darius had suffered at Marathon. He advised Xerxes to wait, and to think, and not to make too hasty a decision:

Seest thou how God with his lightning smites always the bigger animals, and will not suffer them to wax insolent, while those of a lesser bulk chafe him not? How likewise his bolts fall ever on the highest houses and the tallest trees? So plainly does He love to bring down everything that exalts itself. . . . Again, hurry always always brings about disasters, from which huge sufferings are wont to arise; but in delay lie many advantages, not apparent (it may be) at first sight, but such as in course of time are seen of all. Such then is my counsel to thee, O king!

Xerxes was furious with his uncle for his statements. Accusing Artabanos of cowardice, Xerxes informed him that, when the time came for war, he would not be allowed to accompany the army—he would have to stay home with the women. Stating firmly that the time for war had arrived, Xerxes dismissed the council.

That night, however—according to Herodotus—Xerxes began to have doubts. He became convinced that his uncle was right, and that he should abandon his dream of invading Greece. When he fell asleep, he had a dream in which a tall and beautiful man urged him forward in his plans, telling him, "The course that thou didst determine on during the day, let it be followed."

The next morning, the king informed no one of his dream. Yet, when he called the Persians together, he informed them that he had changed his mind. "Understand then that I have changed my intent with respect to carrying war into Greece, and cease to trouble yourselves." The Persians, glad at his change of heart, fell down at Xerxes' feet to show their respect and obedience.

That night, Xerxes had a second dream. The same man spoke to him, telling Xerxes that if he didn't go ahead with the invasion, his days were numbered. "Know therefore and be well assured, that unless thou go forth to the war, this thing shall happen unto thee—as thou are grown mighty and powerful in a short space, so likewise shalt thou within a little time be brought low indeed."

Terrified, Xerxes sent a messenger to retrieve his uncle Artabanos, who came immediately. Xerxes told him of his dream and what the man threatened. He then asked his uncle to help him perform a test. He requested that his uncle wear Xerxes' robes, sit on his throne, and sleep in his bed. In that way, Artabanos should—according to Xerxes—have the same dream.

After some hesitation, according to Herodotus, Artabanos gave in to his nephew's request. He put on his nephew's robes, sat on his throne, and slept in his bed. As he slept, there appeared in his dream the same man who had appeared in Xerxes' dream. The man warned him what would happen to Xerxes if he did not go through with his planned invasion, and said that Artabanos would be punished as well for discouraging Xerxes. "In such words, as Artabanos thought, the vision threatened him, and then endeavored to burn out his eyes with red-hot irons. At this he shrieked, and, leaping from his couch, hurried to Xerxes, and sitting down at his side, gave him a full account of the vision, and told Xerxes that he must go ahead with his plans to invade Greece."

The very next morning, Xerxes informed the Persians that he had decided to go forward with the war against Greece. That night, he had one final vision. Herodotus reported:

> The Magi were consulted upon it, and said that its meaning reached to the whole earth, and that all mankind would become his servants. Now the vision which the king saw was this: he dreamt that he was crowned with a branch of an olive-tree, and that boughs spread out from the olive-branch and covered the whole earth; then suddenly the garland, as it lay upon his brow, vanished. So when the magi had thus interpreted the vision, straightway all the Persians who were come together departed to their several governments, where

each displayed the greatest zeal, on the faith of the king's offers. For all hoped to obtain for themselves the gifts which had been promised. And so Xerxes gathered together his host, ransacking every corner of the continent.

The die had been cast: The invasion was going to happen. Xerxes prepared for the next four years, gathering together his army and supplies. If he won, his father would be avenged, and Xerxes, king of kings, would be the greatest king the world had ever known.

CHAPTER

6

Xerxes Prepares for War

IN THE SUMMER AND AUTUMN OF THE YEAR 481 B.C., XERXES GATHERED his armies together for the invasion of Greece. The army of the eastern satrapies was gathered in Critalla of Cappadocia and was led by Xerxes himself to Sardis, the base camp in Lydia, in the winter of 480 B.C. In early spring, the army moved to Abydos, where it joined the army of the western satrapies.

Herodotus lists 46 nations that supplied troops for Xerxes' army. Persians, Medes, Cissians, Hyrcanians, Assyrians, Bactrians, Indians, Caspians, Arabians, Ethiopians, Armenians, Lydians, and many others combined to make up one of the largest armies the world has ever seen.

Serious questions remain, though, as to how large Xerxes forces actually were. Herodotus claimed that when the numbers of the infantry (1.75 million), cavalry (80,000), fleet crew (517,610), Arab and Libyan allies, Greek allies, and support troops were added up, the total number of men that Xerxes brought to Greece was 5,283,220 (not to mention the 20,000 chariots and camels!).

Most modern historians reject those numbers. They claim that Herodotus greatly exaggerated the numbers of the Persian force in order to make the Greek victory seem all that more impressive. These historians feel that it would have been physically impossible to find and support such a large number of men. Lack of available water alone would make that vast number of troops highly unlikely. Thus, they believe that a more realistic number of troops was in the 200,000 to 250,000 range.

Yet, however many troops there were, it was still one of the mightiest armies of ancient times. The army included a select band of the best warriors in Persia that the Greeks called "the Immortals." Whenever one of them was killed, he was immediately replaced, so the total number of Immortals was never less than 10,000. All of the Immortals were Persian cavalrymen.

Along with the Immortals were 1,000 veterans, handpicked for the battalion responsible for protecting Xerxes. They were easily identified by the golden apples or pomegranates on the butts of their spears. Their numbers were augmented by the Persian cavalry and large numbers of archers.

The Persian soldiers in the field wore sleeved tunics, covered with embroidery, with iron plates like fish scales sewn on for armor. The uniform also included heavy pants, a soft felt cap to protect their heads from the sun, a wicker shield effective against both a javelin and arrows, and a short spear and dagger.

Xerxes, king of kings, rode to battle in a large chariot pulled by the fastest and finest horses in the empire. Chariots were also used by his Lydian troops, and the Indian troops used trained asses as well as horses. Some of the chariots had sharp scythes attached to the hubs of the wheels, which could be used by a skilled driver to cut the wheel spokes of an enemy chariot in two. Arabs on camels rode at the rear, so as not to frighten the horses. The troops, gathering together, must have been an impressive and awe-inspiring sight.

MOVING INTO PLACE

Before he could lead his troops from Persia, Xerxes needed to plan the route his soldiers would travel. The lands from Persia, through the western part of Asia Minor as well as the Asian side of the Aegean and the northern shores of the Aegean, were safely in Persian hands—there would be no serious fighting until his troops approached Athens.

His plan, then, was to move his army across the Hellespont (the strip of water, now called the Dardanelles, that separates Asia from Europe) through Macedonia and Thessaly into Greece. Accompanying the army along the coast was a squadron of ships, transports, and galleys that carried the army's arms, supplies, and luggage.

Crossing the Hellespont was the first obstacle. A bridge was to be built for this purpose, made up of Egyptian and Phoenician ships. Mount Athos was the second major physical obstacle. Not forgetting the disastrous storm that destroyed Darius's navy when it traveled around the peninsula, Xerxes ordered a canal to be built *through* the peninsula, large enough to fit two ships at a time, which would protect his ships and allow them to avoid the perilous journey around Cape Athos. (In later Greek literature, the raising of the massive army and fleet, the construction of the Hellespont bridge, and the digging of the channel in Athos were seen as a sign of hubris by the Persians, an act of great arrogance that was to be punished by the Gods.)

Finally, after months of preparation, Xerxes and his army were ready to move. He and his troops left his capital of Susa, and advanced toward Asia Minor to meet up rest of his army at the western capital of Sardis. Along the way, when they were

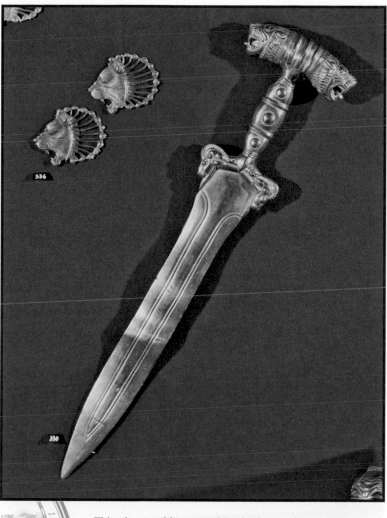

This short golden sword is similar to those carried by the ranks of infantryman in the Persian army. Along with this sword, men would also carry a quiver full of arrows, a bow, and a spear.

entering the town of Celaenae, he met a man named Pythius. His encounters with this man illustrate both the best and worst of Xerxes' character. Herodotus described it as follows:

Now, there lives in this city a certain Pythius, the son of Atys, a Lydian. This man entertained Xerxes and his whole army in a most magnificent fashion, offering at the same time to give him a sum of money for the war. Xerxes, upon the mention of money, turned to the Persians who stood by and asked them, "Who is this Pythius, and what wealth has he, that he could venture on such an offer as this?" They

The Hellespont-Dardanelles

The strait—once known as the Hellespont and today known as the Dardanelles—has long played a strategic role in history. The ancient city of Troy was located just to the west of the entrance to the strait, on the Asiatic side. The strait's Asiatic shore was the focus of the Trojan War. Both Xerxes' Persian army and, later, the Macedonian army of Alexander the Great crossed the Dardanelles, albeit in opposite directions, to invade each other's lands. The strait was vital to the defense of Constantinople (today's Istanbul) during the Byzantine period. Since the fourteenth century, it has been controlled almost continuously by the Turks.

The Russians sought and failed to gain control of the strait during the nineteenth century. The Allies made a failed attempt to seize the Dardanelles during World War I, trying to force the Ottoman Empire out of the war. The Battle of Gallipoli damaged the career of Winston Churchill, who promoted the use of Royal Navy battleships to force open the strait—a gambit that ultimately failed.

Since the Montreux Convention of 1936, the strait has been treated as an international shipping lane, but Turkey retains the right to restrict the naval traffic of non-Black Sea nations (e.g., Greece and Algeria). During World War II, when Turkey was neutral, the Dardanelles were closed to the ships of the belligerent nations for almost the entire war.

answered him, ". . . he is the wealthiest man we know of all in the world, excepting thee."

Xerxes marveled at these last words; and now, addressing Pythius with his own lips, he asked him what the amount of his wealth really was. Pythius answered as follows . . .

Pythius declared to Xerxes that he was worth 2,000 talents of silver and 4 million Daric staters. He then offered all of his money to Xerxes to help with the war effort.

This . . . charmed Xerxes, and he replied, "Dear Lydian, since I left Persia there is no man but thou who has either desired to entertain my army, or come forward of his own free will to offer me a sum of money for the war. Thou has done both one and the other. In return, this is what I will bestow on thee. Thou shalt be my sworn friend from this day. Continue to enjoy all that thou hast acquired hitherto; and be sure to remain ever such as thou now art. If thou dost, thou wilt not repent of it so long as thy life endures."

Xerxes left the city of Celaenae, marching toward Sardis. Along the way, he was given terrible news: A storm had arisen on the Hellespont, destroying the bridge that he had so carefully built.

He was furious. How dare the elements, the air and the water, defy the wishes of Xerxes, the king of kings? Herodotus described his response:

So when Xerxes heard of it he was full of wrath, and straightway gave orders that the Hellespont should receive three hundred lashes. . . . It is certain that he commanded those who scourged the waters to utter, as they lashed them, these barbarian and wicked words: "Thou bitter water, thy lord lays on thee this punishment because thou hast wronged him without a cause, having suffered no evil at his hands.

Verily King Xerxes will cross thee, whether thou wilt or no. Well dost thou deserve that no man should honor thee with sacrifice; for thou art of a truth a treacherous and unsavory river." While the sea was thus punished by his orders, he likewise commanded that the overseers of the work should lose their heads.

The bridges were rebuilt, and, finally, Xerxes was ready to leave the meeting point at Sardis and proceed to Greece. As he got ready to start the march, he was approached by Pythius the Lydian, who had a favor to ask. Emboldened by Xerxes' previous kindness, Pythius explained to Xerxes that he had five sons, and that all five were part of Xerxes' army. Would it be possible, he begged, for his eldest son—his favorite—to remain safe at home with him? Xerxes, according to Herodotus, responded angrily:

> "Thou wretch! darest thou speak to me of thy son, when I am myself on the march against Greece, with sons, and brothers, and kinsfolk, and friends? Thou, who art my bond-slave, and art in duty bound to follow me with all thy household, not excepting thy wife. . . . For thyself and four of thy five sons, the entertainment which I had of thee shall gain protection; but as for him to whom thou clingest above the rest, the forfeit of his life shall be thy punishment." Having thus spoken, forthwith he commanded those to whom such tasks were assigned, to seek out the eldest of the sons of Pythius, and having cut his body asunder to place the two halves, one on the right, and the other on the left, of the great road, so that the army might march out between them.
>
> Then the king's orders were obeyed; and the army marched out between the two halves of the carcass.
>
> First of all went the baggage-bearers, and the sumpter-beasts, and then a vast crowd of many nations mingled together without any intervals, amounting to more than one

half of the army. After these troops an empty space was left, to separate between them and the king. In front of the king went first a thousand horsemen, picked men of the Persian nation—then spearmen a thousand, likewise chosen troops, with their spear-heads pointing towards the ground . . . next ten of the sacred horses called Nisaean . . . then the holy chariot. . . . Next to his came Xerxes himself, riding in a chariot drawn by Nisaean horses, with his charioteer, Patriamphes, the son of Otanes, a Persian, standing by his side.

Thus rode forth Xerxes from Sardis—but he was accustomed every now and then, when the fancy took him, to alight from his chariot and travel in a litter. Immediately behind the king there followed a body of a thousand spearmen, the noblest and bravest of the Persians, holding their lances in the usual manner—then came a thousand Persian horses, picked men—then ten thousand, picked also after the rest, and serving on foot. . . . Behind the ten thousand footmen came a body of Persian cavalry, likewise ten thousand; after which there was again a void space of as much as two furlongs, and then the rest of the army followed in a confused crowd.

Not all who accompanied Xerxes on his campaign were warriors. Xerxes ordered his entire household—wives, children, and servants—and other family members to accompany him. The Immortals, too, were allowed to bring their favorite women and servants as well. One of the infantry commanders brought along his favorite concubine in a beautifully elegant closed carriage, followed by other carriages that contained her personal attendants.

On that first day's march, the army didn't travel far. It was an old Persian tradition that, on beginning such an expedition, the troops would go only a little way and then set up camp. This would allow anyone who had forgotten something to go back and get it before the army was too far from home.

When Xerxes set up camp, it was not like any military camp you might imagine; instead, it looked like he had rebuilt his palace around him. Xerxes had a separate army of bearers who brought tents and furnishings, gilded tables, and chairs made of silver. No one in the Persian nobility would dream of traveling without their gold and silver tableware and their drinking cups covered with jewels. Valets, tailors, perfumers, weavers, cooks, and many others accompanied the king. As you can imagine, the army of invasion moved forward very slowly.

En route to the Hellespont, Xerxes stopped to make an offering of a thousand oxen at the site of Troy, an ancient, destroyed city on the coast of Asia Minor (now Turkey). The destruction of Troy by the Greeks is told by the author Homer in the eighth-century B.C. epic *The Iliad*.

At Abydos, a town on the Asian coast of the Hellespont, Xerxes had built a throne of white marble on top of a hill near the city. There, he could see the shore below and all of his ships and armies. Herodotus writes, "And now, as he looked and saw the whole Hellespont covered with the vessels of his fleet, and all the shore and every plain about Abydos as full as possible with men, Xerxes congratulated himself on his good fortune; but after a little while he wept."

When asked by his uncle Artabanos why he wept, Xerxes (according to Herodotus) replied, "There came upon me a sudden pity, when I thought of the shortness of man's life, and considered that of all this host, so numerous as it is not one will be alive when a hundred years are gone by."

Artabanos seized upon Xerxes' moment of weakness and sentiment and again begged him to reconsider his plans. He warned him that, with such a sizeable navy, there would be no harbor large enough to provide protection against storms. The army, he warned, would run out of supplies as it got further from home and deeper into enemy territory.

Xerxes ignored the warnings of Artabanos. He gave the orders for the troops to begin crossing the Hellespont. Before the crossing began, Xerxes addressed a group of his best soldiers:

> Persians, I have brought you together because I wished to exhort you to behave bravely, and not to sully with disgrace the former achievements of the Persian people, which are very great and famous. Rather let us one and all, singly and jointly, exert ourselves to the uttermost; for the matter wherein we are engaged concerns the common weal. Strain every nerve, then, I beseech you, in this war. Brave warriors are the men we march against, if report says true; and such that, if we conquer them, there is not a people in all the world which will venture thereafter to withstand our arms. And, now let us offer prayers to the gods who watch over the welfare of Persia, and then cross the channel.

It took a full seven days and seven nights for all of Xerxes' army to cross over the Hellespont from Asia into Europe. There would be no turning back.

THE GREEKS PREPARE

During the period in which Xerxes gathered his army and began moving toward Greece, the Greeks were not sitting idly by, doing nothing. They knew that an attack was coming. Preparations were made, beginning with an initial attempt to unite the different city-states to defend themselves against the common enemy. Because each city-state was determined to retain its independence, the idea of overriding military unity among all the Greek city-states was a difficult concept for them to negotiate.

Indeed, a number of the Greek states had even joined the Persian cause—including many of Greece's more powerful families, such as the Peisistratids, the former dictators of Athens.

The Peisistratids, now living in exile, hoped to share the spoils of a Persian victory and return to a defeated Athens in triumph.

Because most of the civilized world fully expected Persia to defeat the Greeks, other groups decided to support what they saw as the winning side, hoping as well to reap the benefits. Ironically, in the long run, these new allies may have hurt the Persians. Each new ally brought its own ideas about how the war should be run. Xerxes quickly tired of hearing advice from anyone who had contributed soldiers or supplies to his army. He came to the conclusion that the only person he could trust and rely upon for advice was himself.

Xerxes faced another problem, as well. While the Greeks attempted to come together in a unified military force, Xerxes had his own issues with unity and command. An army as large as Xerxes' was, as Morgan Llywelyn described in his book *Xerxes*, "impossibly unwieldy." Despite having a highly developed network of runners and messengers, keeping the lines of communication open among such a vast number of people was next to impossible. How would Xerxes know everything that was happening to his army? How could orders be given? Perhaps more importantly, how could orders be changed as the situation required?

GEOGRAPHY

The Greeks used the shape of the land to determine their best defense against the Persian onslaught. Because Greece is mountainous, the Greeks would have to defend the mountain passes that the Persians were expected to use. A place called Thermopylae—a narrow pass located between the mountains of central Greece and the Gulf of Lamia (now called the Gulf of Maliakos)—could, it was felt, be defended by a relatively small force. The Greek generals felt that Thermopylae, as well as the pass through the Vale of Tempe, a valley near Mount Olympus in northeastern Greece, should be the first line of defense.

The noted Athenian statesman Themistocles disagreed with this strategy. He had been instrumental in the building of Athens' navy and advocating a policy of naval expansion. Themistocles had persuaded his countrymen to build 200 triremes (three-tiered, oared warships) with the money from a newly discovered silver mine at Laureion.

He argued that, because the Persians so outnumbered the Greeks, it would be best to concentrate on naval strategy to achieve victory. He felt that the Greeks would do best to fight the Persians in the narrow seas and straits along the Greek coastline. There, the Greeks—with their smaller, more maneuverable warships—would have the advantage.

While the Greeks argued strategy, the Persians drew ever closer. At Dorsicus, the army and the naval fleet were united. According to Herodotus, Xerxes held a review of his forces:

> Now when the numbering and marshalling of the host was ended, Xerxes conceived a wish to go himself throughout the forces, and with his own eyes, behold everything. Accordingly he traversed the ranks seated in his chariot, and, going from nation to nation, made manifold inquiries, while his scribes wrote down the answers; till at last he had passed from end to end of the whole land army, both the horsemen and likewise the foot. This done, he exchanged his chariot for a Sidonian galley, and, seated beneath a golden awning, sailed along the prows of all his vessels (the vessels having now been hauled down and launched into the sea), while he made inquires again, and caused the answers to be recorded by his scribes.

Obviously, Xerxes would leave nothing to chance. Unlike his father, he was determined to personally manage every aspect of the military invasion.

It took the Persians three and a half months to travel unopposed from the Hellespont to Therme, a journey of 360 miles.

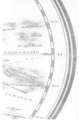

A bronze of Greek soldier and statesman Themistocles is shown *(above)*. Themistocles believed that the key to beating back Xerxes from Greek territories was to battle him at sea. Themistocles thought his ships could do more damage to Xerxes's offensive forces than the Greek defense.

There, food had been sent from Asia for several years previously in preparation for the campaign. Animals had been bought and fattened to prepare them for slaughter. The local populations had been ordered for several months to grind grains into flour.

At Therme, the fleet once again rejoined the army. From there, the Persian fleet traveled down the coast, capturing a few Greek ships that were sent to monitor its movements. The fleet fell into a storm off Mount Pelion, between Casthanaia and Cape Sepias, which caused the loss of one-third of the fleet (according to Herodotus). The Greeks saw this as the punishment of the gods, and it reportedly lifted the morale of the Greek forces. Battered by the storm, the Persian fleet rested at Aphetes.

FIRST MOVEMENTS

A delegation from Thessaly arrived to speak at the League Congress in Athens. Looking for Greek support of the northernmost Greek states, they urged the league to send military forces to block the Persians. They suggested that a strong force should be sent to hold the Tempe gorge, between Ossa and Olympus, a few miles north of the Macedonian border. If this was done, the league was told, the Thessians would stand in strong support.

Because of their pleas, a force of 10,000 hoplites was sent north to hold the Tempe gorge. Dressed in bronze armor and carrying shorter spears than the Persian issue, the force was led by Fuentes and a somewhat reluctant Themistocles. They arrived at Tempe well before Xerxes' forces and dug themselves in to protect the pass, but they were supported by very few Thessalonian horsemen.

Xerxes, learning of this opposition, decided to avoid the Greek troops by moving behind them through the Sarantaporo strait. The Greek forces were warned by Alexander I of Macedon that they were in danger of being cut off and massacred. By the end of May 480 B.C., they marched back south, returning the way they came. All of Thessaly then defected to the Persians, as did many cities north of Thermopylae, when they saw that help was not forthcoming.

At this point, the Persians were still several hundred miles away, and already the Greeks were retreating. The Persians gained allies and strength with every mile they traveled. Xerxes looked unstoppable: How could the Greeks defend themselves against such a powerful foe? At some point, the Greeks would have to stand and fight.

WHERE TO STAND AND FIGHT

Although they were still squabbling about ultimate strategy, the Greeks had finally reached one decision. The Spartans had the strongest tradition of military discipline; the land armies would depend on their leadership. Despite the fact that many Greeks, especially the Athenians, did not agree with the shortsighted plans the Spartans proposed for defense, no one doubted their courage or military skill. Yet, on the very evening of the invasion, the defenders were still divided on strategy.

The Spartans had argued that the defense should be at the Isthmus of Corinth, using that to hold on to the Peloponnesus—not so coincidentally, the location of Sparta. This, in effect, would have surrendered the Greek mainland to the Persians.

Themistocles, an Athenian, saw things differently. Although at first he had gone along with the idea of taking up the defense at Thessaly, he now realized that such a position could not be held. Instead, part of the army would be sent to block the Persian advance at the pass of Thermopylae. King Leonidas of Sparta was put in charge of the effort. It was a gamble—maybe they would be able to stop the Persian advance. Perhaps they could slow down the advance while their navy defeated the Persian navy. Nobody, in fact, knows exactly why this strategy was decided upon.

As always, though, Herodotus had his own opinion:

The force with Leonidas was sent forward by the Spartans in advance of their main body, that the sight of them might encourage the allies to fight, and hinder them from going over to the Persians, as it was likely they might have done had they seen that Sparta was backward. They intended presently, when they had celebrated the Carneian festival (a holiday in honor of the Apollo Carneius) which was now what kept them at home, to leave a garrison in Sparta, and hasten in full force to join the army. The rest of the allies also intended to act similarly; for it happened that the Olympic festival fell exactly at this same period. None of them looked to see the contest at Thermopylae decided so speedily; wherefore they were content to send forward a mere advanced guard. Such accordingly were the intentions of the allies.

In other words, according to Herodotus, the Spartans sent a small force to "hold the fort" until the Carneian festival was over and the rest of the troops could join the fight. No one could have possibly known, or foreseen, that the battle of Thermopylae would become one of the most famous battles in military history.

Thermopylae

BY JULY 480 B.C., THE ALLIED GREEK FLEET WAS ANCHORED IN POSITION at Artemisium, a port on the northeastern shore of Euboea. Euboea sat at the entrance to the Euboean channel that led to the Gulf of Lamia. The fleet now numbered 270 triremes. One hundred of these ships were Athenian, paid for with Larium silver.

By the beginning of August, Leonidas and his men were assembled at Thermopylae. With him were 300 of the finest Spartan hoplites and approximately 6,000 other men, including large contingents of Thebans and Thespians (from the Greek cities of Thebes and Thespiae). They were supported by an additional 1,000 Phocians who knew the terrain and were assigned to help defend the high, narrow track that flanked the pass. Obviously, this was a tiny force to hold back the massive Persian tide.

THE SPARTANS

If anyone could stand up to the Persian onslaught, it would be the Spartans. Stories of their bravery and courage are legend. From childhood, they were trained and educated to be soldiers. The ordinary Spartan was a warrior, trained to obey and endure.

Until the age of seven, Spartan boys were educated at home and taught by their nurses to fight fear. Their official training was then undertaken by the state in the *agoge* system and supervised by the *paidonomos*, an official appointed for that purpose. Their training mainly involved physical exercises; education in music and literature took a secondary position to physical training and endurance. There were even contests to see who could take the most severe flogging, a test known as *diamastigosis*.

At the age of 13, young men were arranged into groups and sent off into the countryside with nothing. There, they were expected to survive solely on their wits and cunning. It was assumed that they would steal their food, but anyone caught stealing was severely punished. Many speculate that this was to teach the young Spartans stealth and quickness. If you were caught, you were assumed not quick or silent enough. This was called the *Crypteia* (secret) ritual.

The Spartans had a story of a boy and a fox. A young Spartan hid a stolen fox under his woolen garment, called a *chlamys*, worn by young men year-round in ancient Greece. When the boy fell under suspicion, he refused to admit that he had stolen the fox. Instead, he stood silently—holding the fox under his chlamys—while all the while it tore at his body with its claws and teeth, until it finally wounded him fatally. The youth became a Spartan hero, held up to young men as an example of

Spartan courage. This was the sort of warrior who waited for Xerxes at Thermopylae.

Even still, the Spartan general Leonidas was convinced that he and his men were going to meet their deaths at Thermopylae. He selected as fighters only men who had sons old enough to take over the family responsibilities should the father die. The Roman writer Plutarch mentions in his *Sayings of Spartan Women* that when Gorgo—the wife of Leonidas—asked her husband what she should do when he left, he replied, "Marry a good man, and have good children."

THE BATTLE BEGINS

While the Persian armies approached Thermopylae, the battle for the sea was already beginning. On August 12, 480 B.C., the Persian fleet arrived at Artemisium. The next morning, the Persian fleet was attacked not by Greek ships, but by a terrible storm. The Persians were trapped for three days, riding at anchor along the beaches of Magnesia. A number of their ships were destroyed. When the Greek fleet returned after fleeing the storm, they were shocked to see that the Persian fleet still outnumbered them by a margin of five to three. The sheer size of the enemy force frightened and demoralized the Greeks. Many of them would have fled had it not been for the persuasive powers of Themistocles.

On August 18, the naval Battle of Artemisium was fought. The battle, while fierce, was indecisive and ended in a draw. The fact that the Greeks held their own against the larger Persian fleet did much to raise the spirits of the Greek forces. Still, two days later, Xerxes ordered a general attack, and nearly half of the Greek ships were damaged. The fleet was forced to withdraw. Despite the importance of this battle, it pales in significance to a battle that occurred at the same time: Thermopylae.

The main pass into southern Greece from the north was known as Thermopylae, and it was there a decisive battle between Xerxes and the Greeks took place.

THERMOPYLAE

It is important to understand the layout of the battlefield. At the time, the pass of Thermopylae consisted of a track along the shore of the Gulf of Malis. This track was so narrow that only one chariot at a time could pass. On the southern side of the track stood the cliffs; on the north side was the gulf. Along the path ran a series of three constrictions, or gates (*pylai*), and at the center gate stood a short wall that had been erected by the Phocians in the previous century to aid in their defense against Thessalian invasions. The term *Hot Gates,* which is the translation of "Thermopylae," comes from the hot springs that were located there. Thermopylae was the last defensible position standing between the mighty Persian army and the city of Athens.

When the Persian army reached the entrance to Thermopylae, the fearful Greeks held a council meeting. The Peloponnesians advised withdrawing forces to the isthmus and defending only the Peloponnesus there. They knew, of course, that the Persians would have to defeat Athens before they could arrive at the isthmus. Others, including the Phocians and Locrians, advised standing fast at Thermopylae. Leonidas agreed.

Meanwhile, the Persians entered the pass, led by Xerxes. Once he reached the pass, he set up camp and spent three days regrouping his armies and preparing them for the assault. The women who accompanied the army were settled away at a safe distance. Then, Xerxes had his throne carefully positioned to allow him the best possible view of the battlefield.

Xerxes sent a mounted scout into the pass to reconnoiter. The Greeks allowed him to come up to the camp, observe them, and depart. The scout returned to Xerxes and told him the size of the Greek force. He also reported that he had witnessed the Spartans not preparing for battle in any way the Persians knew, but exercising and combing their long hair. Xerxes laughed at the reports. Was this any way for men to prepare for battle?

Not believing what he'd heard, he sent for a Greek in his camp, Demaratus. According to Herodotus, Demaratus informed Xerxes that the Spartans were preparing for battle and that it was their custom "when they are about to hazard their lives, to adorn their heads with care. . . . Thou hast now to deal with the first kingdom and town in Greece, and with the bravest men."

Xerxes found this difficult to believe. According to Plutarch, he sent emissaries to the Greek forces. First, he asked Leonidas to switch sides and promised him that he could be king of all of Greece. Leonidas responded, "If you knew what is good in life, you would abstain from wishing for foreign things. For me it is better to die for Greece than to be monarch over my compatriots."

Xerxes once again asked him to surrender his arms. Leonidas gave the famous answer, "Come take them." This quote has been repeated often by politicians and generals, because it expresses the Greeks' determination to risk a sacrifice rather than to surrender without a fight. Today, it is the emblem of the Greek First Army Corps.

Despite the overwhelming odds against them, Herodotus reports that the Greeks' morale was high. When the Spartan named Dieneces was informed that Persian arrows were so numerous that "such was the number of the barbarians, that when they shot forth their arrows the sun would be darkened by their multitude," Herodotus wrote that he responded, "Our . . . friend brings us excellent tidings. If the Medes darken the sun we shall have our fight in the shade."

The armies faced off without fighting for four whole days. Xerxes, it seems, found it impossible to believe that the Greeks would not retreat in the face of his far superior forces. Finally, on the fifth day, thinking that their firm stand was "mere impudence and recklessness," he ordered the Medes and Cissians to move in, take the Greeks prisoner, and bring them before him.

Xerxes sent in the Medes first, perhaps because of their bravery. Or, perhaps, as the writer Diodorus Siculus suggested, he wanted them to bear the brunt of the fighting. After all, the Medes had fairly recently been conquered by the Persians themselves.

Whatever the reason, those moving in against the Greeks found themselves in a full-frontal assault. Herodotus described it as follows:

Then the Medes rushed forward and charged the Greeks, but fell in vast numbers: others however took the places of the slain, and would not be beaten off, though they suffered terrible losses. In this way it became clear to all, and especially to the king, that though he had plenty of combatants, he had but very few warriors. The struggle, however, continued during the whole day.

The Medes quickly discovered that the Greeks had camped on either side of the rebuilt Phocian wall. The fact that it was guarded shows that the Greeks used it to establish a reference line for the battle but then fought in front of it.

Obviously, we will never know with great accuracy what tactics were used. It is thought that the Greeks probably deployed in a phalanx, a wall of overlapping shields and layered spearpoints, which spanned the entire width of the pass. According to Herodotus, the units for each city-state were kept together.

The Persians, armed with arrows and short spears, could not break through the long spears of the Greek phalanx. Additionally, their lightly armored men were no match for the superior armor, weapons, and discipline of the Greek hoplites.

There are indications, however, that the Greeks did not always fight in close formation. They utilized a plan of attack called the *feint* to draw the Medes in; the men would pretend to retreat in disarray, only to turn suddenly and attack the pursuing Medes. In this way, they killed so many Medes that, according to Herodotus, "Xerxes, who was watching the battle, thrice leaped from the throne on which he sat, in terror for his army." According to Ctesias, the first wave of Medes numbered 10,000 soldiers. (Remember that there were only 6,000 Greeks defending the pass.)

The king withdrew the Medes. Now that he knew how hard the Greeks would fight, he sent in his best troops for the second wave of assault: the Immortals. On his side, Leonidas had arranged a system of relays between the hoplites of the various cities so that fresh troops would constantly be sent to the front line. The Persian Immortals, able to approach the Greek lines in only the small numbers that the space allowed, fared no better than the Medes. Xerxes was forced to withdraw them, as well. It is likely that the first day of battle ended there.

Xerxes' assault—his grand army—had failed. Perhaps one reason is that the sheer number of dead bodies broke up and obstructed the Persian line and helped to break their morale. Climbing over the bodies of their dead fellow soldiers and friends, the men saw that they had stepped into a killing machine and were unable to easily withdraw.

This provided Xerxes with yet another reason why the Greeks must be defeated. If these stubborn people could not be dominated, Xerxes was certain that their radical ideas and independent spirit would travel throughout the entire Persian Empire. If that happened, the empire itself would be in danger. The Greeks would have to be defeated.

Faced with the knowledge that a head-on confrontation was doomed to failure, Xerxes would have to find another approach. Fortunately for him, and unfortunately for the Greeks, he would find one.

BETRAYAL

Late on the second day of battle, as Xerxes considered what to do next, good fortune fell into his lap. A Malian named Ephilates informed him of a path that went *around* Thermopylae, and offered to guide them. By taking this path, the Persians could reach the rear of the Greek defenses. The Greeks would then be surrounded and unable to retreat. They would be trapped in the same pass that they had been successfully defending.

Why would Ephilates betray his country? Like many other traitors, Ephilates was motivated by his desire for a reward.

After the war ended, however, Ephilates was unable to reap the reward of his traitorous actions. He was forced to live in exile and was ultimately assassinated.

The path led from east of the Persian camp along the ridge of Mount Anopaea, behind the cliffs that ran along the side of the pass. It then branched in two directions: One path led to Phocis, the other down to the Gulf of Malis at Alpenius. Leonidas had stationed 1,000 Phocian volunteers on the heights to guard this path.

For all the Greeks' preparations and insistence on a defense at Thermopylae, they were not prepared for this. There were no advance positions, sentinels, or patrols. Their first warning of the approach of the Immortals under the command of Hydranes was the rustling of oak leaves on the morning of the third day of the battle. Herodotus said that they "jumped up and flew to seize their arms," perhaps indicating that they had been asleep.

Not wishing to be delayed by a long assault, Hydranes resorted to a tactic that turned out to be a winning one: He fired "showers of arrows" at them. The Phocians quickly retreated to the crest of the mountain, ready to make their last stand. The Persians, though, "not thinking it worth their while to delay on account of Phocians," passed on and branched left to Alpenus. For this act of treason, the name Ephilates earned a lasting stigma—it means "nightmare" and is synonymous with "traitor" in Greek (not dissimilar to the use of "Benedict Arnold" in the United States).

THE FINAL STAND

Leonidas was not surprised by the actions of the Persians. He had been kept informed of their every move from a variety of sources, and he received the first intelligence of the outflanking movement before dawn. When he learned that the Phocians had not held, he called a council. Dawn was just breaking.

Some of the Greeks wished to leave; others wanted to stay. At the end of the council, some of the men departed. Herodotus believed that Leonidas himself blessed their departure, ordering them to go, but he also related the other point of view, that they left without orders. The 300 Spartans had pledged themselves to fight to the death, and the Thebans were held hostage against their will. A group of approximately 700 Thespians, led by General Demophilus, the son of Diadromes, refused to leave with the other Greeks and decided to remain with the Spartans.

The Spartans stayed true to their oath to the Oracle at Delphi in their decision to stand and fight. According to Herodotus, the city of Sparta had consulted the oracle before the warriors set out to fight. The oracle made the following prophecy in hexameter verse:

> O ye men who dwell in the streets of broad Lacedaemon!
> Either your glorious town shall be sacked by the children of
>   Perseus,
> Or, in exchange, must all through the whole Laconian
>   country
> Mourn for the loss of a king, descendant of great Heracles.
> He cannot be withstood by the courage of bulls nor of lions,
> Strive as they may; he is as might as Jove; there is naught
>   that shall stay him,
> Till he have got for his prey your king, or your glorious city.

In essence, the oracle warned that either Sparta would be conquered and left in ruins, or one of her two hereditary kings must sacrifice his life to save her. There was yet another reason for the Spartans to stand fast besides the oracle's prediction: It made good military sense to delay the advance of the Persians and to cover the retreat of the remainder of the Greek army.

At dawn on August 20, the two sides prepared for the final battle. Xerxes made his libations at sunrise and then waited until

After a betrayal by Ephilates, a Greek soldier, King Leonidas remained in the pass of Thermopylae with a small number of soliders and slaves. True to their training, their reputation, and a famous prophecy, 300 Spartan soldiers fought bravely and to their deaths, even managing to kill two of Xerxes' brothers.

he thought that the Immortals had enough time to descend the mountain. Leonidas and the remaining 1,500 men, including the 300 Spartans, courageously awaited their fate.

Xerxes gave the order to advance. This time, the Greeks came out from behind the wall to meet them in the wider part of the pass, with a view toward slaughtering as many Persians as they could. They fought with spears until their spears were shattered and then switched to short swords (*xiphoi*). During the struggle, Herodotus tell us that two brothers of Xerxes— Abrocomes and Hyperanthes—were killed. Leonidas himself died in the assault. The Spartans fought tirelessly to keep Leonidas's body from falling into the hands of the Persians.

When they received information that Ephilates and the Immortals were coming up from behind, the Greeks withdrew and took a stand on a small hill behind the wall. Herodotus described the end:

> Here they defended themselves to the last, such as still had swords using them, and the others resisting with their hands and teeth; till the barbarians, who in part had pulled down the wall and attacked them in front, in part had gone round and now encircled them upon every side, overwhelmed and buried the remnant which was beneath showers of missile weapons (arrows, javelins and stones).

Storming through the now undefended pass, the Persians stepped over the deep piles of their dead fellow warriors. Several stopped to steal helmets, armor, and swords from the corpses. There was little time to enjoy the victory: next was an attack on Athens itself.

After the battle, Xerxes came down from his throne to inspect the battlefield. Imagine his shock and dismay at seeing the bodies of an estimated 20,000 dead Persians littering the ground and then the bodies of the relatively small number of the enemy—perhaps 1,500—that had died standing up to his mighty army. When Xerxes came upon the body of Leonidas of Sparta, he showed great contempt for the leader who had caused him so much more trouble than he had bargained for. As Herodotus tells it, "He ordered that the head should be struck off, and the trunk fastened to a cross. This proves to me most clearly, what is plain in many other ways—namely, that King Xerxes was more angry with Leonidas, while he was still in life, than with any other mortal." Typically, the Persians honored anyone who fought bravely. Xerxes, however—not thinking clearly—was still furious that Leonidas had led the Greeks so bravely and killed so many of Xerxes' army.

The Persians were not allowed time to mourn their dead. The king gave orders that all of the Persian dead would be buried in quickly dug trenches. He left approximately 1,000 Persians unburied; by burying the majority of the bodies, he hoped to hide from the world the high cost of his victory. Xerxes also ordered funerals for his two brothers killed in battle. As soon as those ceremonies were completed, Xerxes ordered his troops forward.

Sometime after the battle, all of the Spartan dead were gathered up by their countrymen and buried under one mound. A stone lion was set up guard them. Their epitaph, composed by the poet Simonides, read, "O passerby, tell our people that we

Thermopylae in Literature and Popular Culture

It is interesting to note that, despite the fact that the Greeks (considered by Westerners to be the "good guys") lost the battle of Thermopylae, the battle itself has become an essential part of our cultural history. It is talked about, shown, and made reference to in poems, novels, movies, and even television shows!

Many famous poets, including Lord Byron, A.E. Housman, T.S. Eliot, Kavafis, Emily Dickinson, and Sylvia Plath, have made reference to the battle. Novels such as *Gates of Fire* by Steven Pressfield and *The Spartan* by Caroline Dale Snedeker have been written about the battle. The graphic novel *300* was made into a movie that was released in 2007. Even on the television show *Star Trek: Deep Space Nine*, Dr. Julian Bashir offered to take Ezri Dax on a date in a holosuite program that depicted the Battle of Thermopylae!

lie here obeying their orders." The stone lion is no longer there, but the epitaph was engraved on a new stone erected in 1955.

The defeat at Thermopylae was a disaster for the Greeks, losing them effective control of the center of the mainland. Stunned by the news, Themistocles ordered a full retreat of the Greek fleet from Artemesium on the night of August 20. With the Greek defensive line lost, the Persians were now in a position to quickly move southward, conquer Athens, and take control of the remainder of the mainland. It looked as if Xerxes' dream of conquering Greece was becoming a reality.

CHAPTER

8

Xerxes Goes in for the Kill

FOLLOWING THE DEFEAT AT THERMOPYLAE, THE WHOLE OF THE GREEK mainland lay in the path of Xerxes' army. The terrified Greek populace began to evacuate from the Persian onslaught, and the Greek command tried to settle on a strategy for where they should make their next stand.

Leading the Greek fleet from Artemisium, Themistocles headed toward Salamis to assist with the evacuation of Athens. He left inscriptions on springs of water along the way, addressed to the Ionian Greek crews of the Persian fleet, that said:

Men of Ionia, that what you are doing [working for the Persians] is not proper, campaigning against your fathers

94

and wishing to enslave Greece. It would be best if you came to our side.

Meanwhile, reports reached Athens about the devastation that Xerxes and his armies were inflicting on the Greek countryside. The Persian army burned and sacked the cities of Plataea and Thespiae. The Athenians would have to evacuate their city and move to safer ground.

At this time, many Greeks felt that they had little choice but to pull back as far as the Isthmus of Corinth and defend the Peloponnese from there. Themistocles felt differently. He persuaded Eurybiades to anchor the Greek fleet at Salamis, an island off the western coast of Attica. The Athenian reserve fleet moved there as well.

Most of the population of Athens fled to Salamis or Aegina, another nearby island. Part of the Persian army approached Athens, and the few remaining citizens attempted to protect the city. Indeed, some Athenians tried to defend the sacred hill of the Acropolis, but the Persians broke through by climbing a path on the hill's steep north side and flanking the defenders, much as they had done at Thermopylae. Having taken the hill, they set fire to the Acropolis. Soon, much of the rest of Athens was in ashes.

For Xerxes, the time looked right to make a final move and crush the Greeks once and for all. It was now September, and winter would be fast approaching. In the winter, transportation problems for the Persian army would greatly increase. Food would become more difficult to find, especially as Xerxes' supply lines grew longer and longer as his troops moved further into Greece.

There was another factor as well. Xerxes had been away from home for months. Like any ruler, he was concerned about events in his own kingdom and within his own court. Although he had able administrators to run things while he was away, he knew from his father's own experiences that a ruler rules best from home. He needed to defeat the Greeks decisively and sail home to Persia as quickly as possible.

WHY SALAMIS?

Xerxes realized that, as long as the Greeks had a naval fleet, his victory was not complete. He saw Salamis as an obvious site for the final battle. This would be a sea battle, and his fleet would have a sizeable numeric advantage.

There were some negatives aspects to this strategy, as well. Xerxes' navy had suffered losses from storms in the Aegean Sea and at Artemisium. Also, Xerxes had not personally witnessed any of the earlier naval battles his fleet had fought with the Greeks. Although he had received reports, the messengers—intimidated by the king—often would strive to make the news sound better than it actually was. It is quite possible that Xerxes never learned the actual number of Persian losses at sea. It is equally possible that the Greek casualties reported to him were greatly exaggerated.

This, of course, is an experience common to many rulers. Assistants and advisors, afraid to tell the ruler any bad news, instead tell him what they think he wants to hear. A ruler, however, cannot make informed decisions based on a slanted view of events. The information supplied to Xerxes could well prove fatal.

Still, Xerxes was certainly no fool. Yet, in trying to run every aspect of the military campaign, he was forced to rely on others for the information he needed to plan his strategy. He became convinced that now was the time to destroy the rebellious Greeks. With a fleet of an estimated 650 to 800 ships, it seemed likely that he could easily defeat the smaller Greek fleet. If that happened, he could quickly occupy the rest of Greece, turning the once independent city-states into satrapies of the Persian Empire.

THE GREEK RESPONSE

Eurybiades and the Spartans continued to argue with Themistocles about the necessity of fighting at Salamis. They wanted

Against advice and warnings, Xerxes ordered his men to charge into the narrow passages between the islands around Salamis, hoping that his large Persian fleet would quickly crush the Greek navy. Underestimating the resolve of the Greeks after they had seen his forces ransack their cities and countryside, Xerxes was surprised when his battle plans unraveled before his eyes.

to fight the battle closer to Corinth—which would make it easier to retreat to the mainland, if necessary—or withdraw completely and let the Persians attack them by land. The arguments grew so heated that Eurybiades threatened to strike

Themistocles with his staff of office. Themistocles responded by saying, "Strike then, but hear me!"

His arguments were straightforward. Whereas the Spartans wanted to seal off the Isthmus of Corinth with a wall, preventing the Persians from defeating them on land, Themistocles argued that a wall across the isthmus was pointless as long as the Persian army could be transported and supplied by the Persian navy. His argument was largely based on one particular interpretation of the Oracle at Delphi, which prophesized that Salamis would "bring death to women's sons," but also that the Greeks ultimately would be saved by a "wooden wall." Themistocles chose to interpret the wooden wall as the fleet of ships, and argued that Salamis would bring death to the Persians, not to the Greeks.

Although the Spartans were won over by Themistocles's eloquence, he was still concerned that Eurybiades would overrule him, despite the Spartan's lack of naval expertise. As a result, he came up with a plan to make it impossible for the Greeks to withdraw.

The plan itself is open to historical doubt. It is described in Aeschylus's play *The Persians,* written only eight years after the battle. Herodotus also describes the plan set forth by Themistocles (as does Plutarch), calling it "his celebrated trick with Sicinnus," but some scholars doubt that it actually occurred.

What was reported to have happened was this: Themistocles sent an informer, a slave named Sicinnus—the teacher of his children—to speak to Xerxes. His job was to convince Xerxes that the Greeks had been unable to agree on a location for battle and would quietly retreat during the night. Xerxes believed Sicinnus's story (it is uncertain whether or not he addressed the king directly) and sent his Egyptian squadron to blockade the western outlet of the straits. This would stop any Greek ships that planned to escape. Sicinnus was later given his freedom and granted citizenship as a reward for his role.

Aeschylus's *The Persians*

The Persians, a tragedy by the ancient Greek playwright Aeschylus, is the oldest surviving play in history. It was produced in 472 B.C., along with three other plays, none of which survive. *The Persians* is the sole surviving Greek tragedy that is based on an actual historical event—the Battle of Salamis. That battle took place in 480 B.C., only eight years before the play was produced. Aeschylus had participated in the battle, and it is likely that most of his audience had been directly affected by, if not actually part of, the battle as well.

The play takes place in Susa, the capital of Persia. It opens with the chorus (representing Persian nobles) and Xerxes' mother, Atossa, awaiting news of King Xerxes' expedition against the Greeks. A messenger arrives to deliver word of the defeat, the names of the Persian leaders who have been killed, and the good news that Xerxes has escaped and is returning home. The messenger then gives a graphic description of the battle and its outcome.

The ghost of Darius appears to Atossa and explains that the Persians were defeated because of the hubris (excessive pride and self-confidence) of Xerxes, who built a bridge of boats across the Hellespont and—by doing so—offended the gods. Xerxes himself does not appear until near the end of the play, returning home in defeat and shame. By the time the play has concluded, he realizes the cause of his defeat and ends the play more noble than when it began.

What makes the play so timeless is that Aeschylus did not turn his play into propaganda, attempting to make his audience of Greeks hate the Persians. Instead, he strove to make his audience feel pity for the Persians, the enemy they had so recently defeated. By showing both sides of the battle compassionately, Aeschylus made *The Persians* a work of art that has survived for nearly 2,500 years.

Xerxes did hear one opposing voice. Artemisia, the queen of Halicarnassus in Asia Minor and Xerxes' ally, purportedly attempted to convince him to wait for the Greeks to surrender. She felt that a battle in the straits of Salamis would be deadly to the large Persian ships, which would be outmaneuvered by the smaller, faster Greek vessels. Xerxes was certain of a Persian victory, however, and—along with his advisor Mardonius—decided to go forward with the attack. The Persian ships searched the gulf all night for the Greek retreat, while the Greeks slept comfortably on their ships. During the night, Aristides, formerly a political opponent of Themistocles, reported that the plan had worked, and he allied with the Athenian commander to strengthen the Greek force.

THE BATTLE OF SALAMIS

The next day, at dawn, Xerxes was carried in his canopied chair to the heights above Salamis, from which he could watch the battle. It was customary for royalty to observe battles from the nearest and highest hillside; thus, Xerxes had the best possible view of what he was certain would be a Persian victory.

It is not altogether certain which was the exact day of battle (the Greek Navy celebrates September 12 as Battle of Salamis Day). That morning, the Persians, exhausted from searching for the Greeks all night, were ordered to sail into the strait to attack the Greek fleet. When it became obvious to the Greeks that the battle was approaching, the fleet took to sea and, according to Aeschylus, sang the following song:

> Forward, sons of the Greeks
> Liberate the motherland, liberate
> Your children, your women, the altars of the gods of your
>   fathers
> And the graves of your forebears:
> This is the fight for everything.

The Greek fleet started to row toward the Persians at day-break. When it became obvious that they would meet them at the center of the strait, however, which was wide enough to allow the Persians to use their numerical advantage, the Greeks began to retreat. According to Plutarch, this was done not only to gain better position but also to gain some time until the early morning wind began. The fleet positioned itself so that it was covered on the left by the islet of St. George and on the right by the peninsula of Kynosoura. At this point, according to Aeschylus, a ghost woman appeared and shouted, "Until when are you Greeks going to retreat?" The morning wind arose, shaking the tall Phoenician ships. The ship of the Athenian Ameinias of Pallene rammed the leading Persian ship. The rest of the Greeks joined the attack.

Xerxes, observing the battle from high above, quickly saw the trap that his ships had been lured into. He sent runners to order his fleet to pull back, but it was too late. The battle was under way, and there was nothing that Xerxes could do.

It is easy to imagine the king's feelings as he observed the battle. Perhaps, he might have thought, it was wrong to think that the Greeks were too cowardly to fight. If he had not been so confident, so assured of victory, he might have taken more time to plan and to think of alternate strategies. Xerxes should have realized that the Greeks were fighting for their country, for their independence. These were people who were determined to fight and win.

As the battle carried on, the Greek and Persian ships continued to ram each other. Both sides had marines on their ships (the Greeks were fully armed hoplites), and arrows and javelins flew across the narrow strait. The waves caused the archers on the Phoenician ships to miss their targets, giving the advantage to the hoplites, who fought hand to hand. In addition, the Greek triremes were outfitted with an *embolon*, a long bronze protrusion fitted to the prow at water level. This enabled the Greeks to ram and sink enemy ships far more easily than they could be sunk themselves.

As the sun rose higher in the sky, the battle quickly escalated. The chief Persian admiral Ariamenes rammed Themistocles's ship. In the hand-to-hand combat that followed, a Greek marine killed Ariamenes; confusion then erupted among the Persians, because the chain of command was broken. The encircled Persians tried to turn back, but the strong morning wind was behind them—they were trapped. Those who were able to turn around were blocked by the rest of the Persian fleet, which had jammed into the strait.

Less than a mile of water separated the island of Salamis from the shore held by the Persian infantry. Yet, as the day went on and the battle continued, Xerxes was powerless to save his fleet. He saw how the Athenians had succeeded in working around his own ships, using his vast numbers against him with their faster, more maneuverable Greek fleet. He could only watch in horror as his fleet and all of his dreams of the conquest of Greece were destroyed.

In his play *The Persians*, Aeschylus described the scene of the battle from the Persian point of view:

> Crushed hulls lay upturned on the sea so thick
> You could not see the water, choked with wrecks
> And slaughtered men; while all the shores and reefs
> Were strewn with corpses. Soon in wild disorder
> All that was left of our fleet turned tail and fled.
> But the Greeks pursued us, and with oars all broken
> Fragments of wreckage split the survivors' heads
> As if they were tunneys or a haul of fish:
> And shrieks and wailing rang across the water
> Till nightfall hid us from them.

At least 200 Persian ships were sunk, including one by Artemisia. Finding herself pursued by a Greek ship, she attacked

In a monumental defeat for Xerxes, the Greeks lured and trapped the Persian fleet in the Battle of Salamis. With their small ships and soldiers skilled in hand-to-hand combat, the Greeks destroyed the Persian forces with clever battle tactics and sheer determination to remain free from Xerxes' rule.

and rammed a Persian vessel, and then convinced the captain of the Greek ship that she too was Greek. He quit the chase.

It is said that the Immortals, the elite Persian royal guard, had to evacuate to the small island of Psyttaleia after their ships sank and were all slaughtered. According to Herodotus, the Persians suffered many more casualties than the Greeks because most Persians did not know how to swim. One of the Persian casualties was yet another brother of Xerxes. Those Persians who survived and made it to shore were killed by the Greeks who found them.

Xerxes, watching from his golden throne, saw it all. He remarked, according to Herodotus, that Artemisia was the only general to show any true bravery by ramming nine Athenian triremes. "My female general has become a man," he said, "and all my male generals women."

When some Phoenicians approached Xerxes and blamed the Ionians for cowardice during battle, Xerxes—who had witnessed the battle and the courage of the Ionian fleet—had the Phoenicians beheaded. He did this, according to Herodotus, "to prevent them from casting the blame for their own misconduct upon braver men."

AFTERMATH

The victory of the Greeks marked the turning point in the Persian Wars. The Battle of Salamis, called the first great naval battle in history, was a complete disaster for the Persian forces. Even though the Greeks were badly outnumbered, they had managed to destroy nearly half of the Persian fleet while losing only about 40 of their own ships.

With the destruction of the Persian fleet came the end of Xerxes' dream to bring the Greeks into the Persian Empire. Facing the Persian threat, Athens and Sparta, as well as other smaller city-states, had united for a common cause. They learned that they were not just Athenians or Spartans—they were Greeks, sharing common bonds of language, customs, and culture. This new idea of a Greek nation helped lead the way to the Golden Age of Greece that followed later.

The Battle of Salamis has been described by many major historians (including Donald Kagan and John Keegan) as the single most significant battle in human history. The Greek victory protected the emergence of the Greek concept of democracy and individual rights and guarded Greek philosophy and culture. The eventual birth and flowering of Western culture as we know it might never have occurred had the Persians defeated Greece; because of the enormous and wide-ranging influence of Western culture on all of humanity, it is quite possible that the world today would be completely and fundamentally different if the Greeks had lost at Salamis.

Although the Greeks were exultant at their victory, Xerxes and the remains of his forces were devastated. What would he do next?

Xerxes Withdraws

AFTER HIS DEFEAT AT SALAMIS, XERXES FOUND HIMSELF IN A DANGEROUS position. Without his navy, he was unable to supply his huge army from relatively resource-poor Greece, so he withdrew his forces to the Hellespont.

His strategy was to march his army back over the bridge of ships he had created, but he needed to do so before the Greeks arrived to destroy it (not knowing that the Greeks had already decided not to do this—they did not want Xerxes and his armies trapped in Europe). As Herodotus phrased it, Xerxes "was afraid lest the Greeks might be counseled by the Ionians, or without their advice might determine to sail straight to the Hellespont and break down the bridges there; in which case he would be blocked up in Europe, and run great risk of perishing." Xerxes ordered the remaining fleet to retreat under cover of night.

The victorious Greeks pursued the Persian ships but made no serious effort to capture them. Themistocles did, however, stop at several islands to collect tribute payments. This served not only to show off the new, powerful Athenian fleet but also to help pay the crews manning those ships.

By late October, Xerxes led the majority of his army back as well—along the road they had traveled just months before, when they were confident of victory. This time, however, he led a beaten and demoralized army. Herodotus described the retreat:

> All along the march, in every country where they chanced to be his soldiers seized and devoured whatever corn they could find belonging to the inhabitants; while, if no corn was to be found, they gathered the grass that grew in the fields, and stripped the leaves, and so fed themselves. They left nothing anywhere, so hard were they pressed by hunger. Plague too and dysentery attacked the troops, while still upon their march, and greatly thinned their ranks. Many died; others fell sick and were left behind in the different cities that lay upon the route.

Xerxes marched from Sessaly to Sestos in just 45 days, arriving shortly before mid-December. The bridges across the Hellespont were in fact down, destroyed by violent storms. The army was ferried across to Abydos by the Persian fleet, which had already arrived. From there, Xerxes marched on to Sardis, where he spent the winter.

Xerxes did not withdraw all of his troops from Greece. He left approximately 30,000 to 50,000 men in Greece, under the command of one of his best generals, his brother-in-law Mardonius. The initial task of these troops was to defend the rear of the Persian army as it retreated from Greece. After that, Xerxes had another goal in mind for the remaining army. His hopes were that this smaller, more tightly organized army would be able to succeed where his massive army had not, and defeat the resistance.

FINAL BATTLES

In the spring of 479 B.C., Mardonius sent his force through Boeotia and Attica to Athens. Through Alexander I of Macedon, Mardonius asked for a truce with Athens, offering them an autonomous government and Persian aid to rebuild their city. Athens, quite understandably, rejected this offer, sending Alexander the following message:

> We know that the Persian strength is many times greater than our own. Nevertheless, such is our love of freedom, that we will defend ourselves in whatever way we can . . . you may tell Mardonius, therefore, that so long as the sun keeps his present course in the sky, we Athenians will never make peace with Xerxes.

Instead, the Athenians appealed to Sparta for help defending the city. The Spartans hesitated, however, because of yet another religious festival. In the end, Chileos of Tegea convinced the Spartans of the danger they would face if Athens was forced to make peace with the Persians.

After hearing of Athens' rejection of his offer, Mardonius decided to subdue the city by force. Once again, Athenians were forced to evacuate their city under the threat of Persian invasion. In June, Mardonius took the city. Learning that the Spartans had sent 45,000 men under the command of Pausanias, he ordered the complete destruction of Athens. He burned or tore down whatever was still standing from the previous Persian invasion and then retreated to Thebes, hoping to lure the Greek army there.

Themistocles was honored as a hero and statesman for his responsibility for the Greek victory against the invading Persians. His efforts to rebuild the Athenian fleet and his battle strategies contributed to Xerxes' retreat, which allowed Greece to remain independent.

There, he arranged his troops in a five-mile-long line just south of Thebes, reaching Plataea. During his retreat from Athens, he ordered the Persian soldiers to leave a path of destruction through the countryside, burning homes and crops and stealing livestock. By doing so, he hoped to destroy the supplies that the Spartan army would need.

Mardonius was also counting on the Greeks to begin quarreling among themselves again and to be unable to unite. This proved to be overly optimistic. The Athenians sent 8,000 men and marched with the Spartan forces toward the plain of Plataea, where the Greek hoplites could fight more easily.

By this time, the Greek army had been reinforced by many other city-states, bringing their total strength up to perhaps 50,000. According to Peter Green in his book *The Greco-Persian Wars*, the size of the Greek army was roughly equivalent to that of the Persian army. Others sources disagree. Herodotus, for instance, claimed 110,000 Greek troops versus 300,000 Persian!

However many troops there were, both armies camped in front of each other for 10 days, with only small raids taking place on each side. Finally, Mardonius decided to attack. That night, according to Herodotus, Alexander of Macedon—a Persian ally—crossed the Asopus River and spoke to the Athenian generals, warning them of the upcoming assault.

> Men of Athens, that which I am about to say I trust to your honor; and I charge you to keep it secret from all excepting Pausanias, if you would not bring me to destruction. Had I not greatly at heart the common welfare of Greece, I should not have come to tell you; but I am myself a Greek by descent, and I would not willing see Greece exchange freedom for slavery.

The Athenians and the Spartans switched positions so that the Athenians would defend against the main Persian force. The Spartans would fight the Greek subjects who served in the Persian army. On that night, the twelfth night, the Greeks started to move. Learning that the Greeks had abandoned their positions, Mardonius addressed his troops. According to Herodotus, he said:

> You yourselves beheld them change their place in the line; and here, as all may see, they have run away in the night. Verily, when their turn came to fight with those who are of truth the bravest warriors in the world, they showed plainly enough that they are men of no worth. . . . Now we must not allow them to escape us, but must pursue after them till we overtake them; and then we must exact vengeance for all the wrongs which have been suffered at their hands by the Persians.

Noting that the Greek formation was divided in three, he decided to attack, unaware that he was sending his forces into a trap. The Persian cavalry and archers first came upon the Spartans, who were still moving, and the infantry arrived soon after. The Spartans retreated higher into the mountains, where they were protected from cavalry attacks. The cavalry and archers did little damage to the Spartans and withdrew when the infantry arrived. The Spartans asked the Athenians for help, but they were unable to send immediate aid because they were being attacked by the Thebans.

The Persians formed a shield wall and fired volleys of arrows at the Spartans and Tegeans. After suffering the arrow onslaught, the Tegeans attacked, forcing the Spartans to follow. The Greeks' long spears gave them a tactical advantage over the Persians' short spears and swords, and the battle soon turned into a slaughter.

The Persians were annihilated. Mardonius himself was killed, his skull crushed by a stone from the hand of a Spartan named Aeimnestus, just as an oracle at the shrine of Amphiaraus had predicted. In the meantime, while the Spartans were still facing Persian arrows, the Athenians moved to help them but found themselves facing the Persians' Greek allies. Although most of these allies decided not to fight against their countrymen and pretended cowardice, the Thebans attacked and fought bravely, pulling back only after they suffered heavy casualties.

The battle was soon over. The Persian Artabazus, who had tried and failed to convince Mardonius to avoid a direct battle, took command of the remnants of the Persian army and immediately retreated, allowing the Greeks to capture their camp. There, the Greeks went to work dividing up the treasures that

Oracle of Delphi

In ancient times, Delphi was the site of the most important oracle in Greece. The Oracle of Delphi was located on the slopes of Mount Parnassus, where there was a temple sacred to Apollo. The Pythia was the priestess presiding over the oracle, and she was credited with delivering prophecies that were inspired by Apollo. She exerted considerable influence throughout Greek culture. The Greeks consulted her prior to all major undertakings, including wars, and the founding of colonies.

Attempts have been made to find a scientific explanation for the Pythia's inspiration. Many researchers believe that her power to see the future—her ability to have "visions"—was linked to vapors from the Castalian Spring that surrounded her. The observation was also made that sessions of prophesy would take place in, or be preceded by a visit to, an enclosed chamber at the base of the temple. It is thought possible that the ethylene gas that seeped in there caused hallucinations in the Pythia, which were then believed to have been visions sent by Apollo.

littered the banks of the Asopus. Peter Green described it in *The Greco-Persian Wars*:

> The result was fantastic; tents with gold and silver furnishings, inlaid couches, bowls, cups and cauldrons, armlets and torques, daggers and scimitars all of pure gold—"not to mention richly embroidered clothes which, amongst so much of greater value, seemed of no account." In addition to this there were concubines, horses, camels, and an infinity of coined money; months afterward the Plataeans were still turning up hidden strong-boxes and treasure-chests.

A bronze column in the shape of intertwined snakes was created from the treasure acquired in the plunder of the Persian camp and was offered at the oracle of Delphi, which commemorated all the Greek city-states that participated in the battle. Part of the column survives, displayed at the Hippodrome in modern Istanbul. Constantine the Great carried it there during the founding of his city (it was once called Constantinople). The column lists all the city-states that took part in the battle, largely confirming Herodotus's account of the event (but not his numbers).

THE AFTERMATH

According to Herodotus, only 43,000 of the 300,000 Persians survived the battle, while the Greeks lost just 159 men. Plutarch claimed that 1,360 Greeks were killed. Given the unreliable and inaccurate estimates of the number of troops involved, it is unlikely that we will ever have a true rendering of the casualties. It is sufficient to understand that the Persians suffered yet another devastating loss.

Tradition has it that, on the same day as the Battle of Plataea, the naval battle of Mycale also took place. In that battle, the Greek fleet destroyed the remains of the Persian fleet in the Aegean Sea off the coast of Ionia. The remains of the Persian

As Xerxes and most of his army returned to Persia, a smaller group of troops were left to fend off attacks against the retreating soldiers and to also regroup and attack Greek forces once again. From the items left behind by the last of this Persian army, the Greeks made a bronze column *(above)* of two snakes, twisted together, and offered it as tribute to the oracle of Delphi.

army under the command of Artabazus tried to retreat back to Asia Minor. Most of the 43,000 survivors were ambushed and killed by the forces of Alexander of Macedon at the estuary of the Strymon River.

This ended the defensive phase of the Persian Wars. Although the Persians continued to interfere in Greek politics, and Greece and Persia would battle occasionally, Persia would never again try to conquer Greece. Indeed, in the fourth century B.C., less than 200 years later, the Persians themselves would be conquered by the Greeks, led by Alexander the Great.

By uniting against a common enemy and fighting off the Persian invasion, the Greeks had gained a sense of identity. Free of the threat of Persian conquest, they were able to turn their attentions inward, which led to the Golden Age of Greece. This flowering of art, philosophy, architecture, literature, and political thought set the stage for all of Western civilization that has since followed.

Xerxes returned home to Persia a weakened king. Bitter and angry at his loss, he was blamed by his people, counselors, and priests for Persia's defeat. The king of kings, beaten and humiliated by a group of small, unorganized city-states, would have to work hard to reestablish his power and authority.

10

Decline and Death

ALTHOUGH XERXES RETURNED TO PERSIA IN DEFEAT, HIS EMPIRE—FOR the moment, at least—remained intact. It was still the largest and richest empire in the world. He brought back to Persia, however, the knowledge of his defeat, an army in tatters, and the fear that his defeat might weaken his hold on the empire.

Even as the retreat began, quarrels sprang up among Xerxes' generals as to who was to blame for the defeat. On the retreat from Mycale, the king's brother Masistes blamed the admiral Artayntes and called him worse than a woman—the deadliest of insults a Persian could give. Artayntes tried to avenge the insult with blood but was stopped by Xenagoras of Halicarnassus, who was rewarded with the rule of all Cilicia for saving the royal brother.

Masistes soon found himself in even graver danger. While Xerxes remained in Sardis, he had fallen love with Masistes' wife. She rejected his unwanted advances, so Xerxes, in an attempt to make her more "friendly," married her daughter Artaynte to his eldest son Darius. This only served to complicate matters.

Herodotus told the tale as follows:

> Accordingly he [Xerxes] betrothed these two persons to one another, and, after the usual ceremonies were completed, took his departure for Susa. When he was come there, and had received the woman into his palace as his son's bride, a change came over him, and, losing all love for the wife of Masistes, he conceived a passion for his son's bride, Masistes' daughter. And Artaynte—for so was she called—very soon returned his love.

Soon enough, things became even more complicated. Xerxes was tricked by Artaynte into giving her a "long robe, of many colors" that Queen Amestris, Xerxes' wife, had woven for him. Herodotus wrote:

> Then Artaynte, who was doomed to suffer calamity together with her whole house, said to him—"Wilt thou indeed give me whatever I like to ask?" So the king, suspecting nothing less than that her choice would fall where it did, pledged his word, and swore to her. She then, as soon as she heard his oath, asked boldly for the robe. Hereupon Xerxes tried all possible means to avoid the gift; not that he grudged to give it, but because he dreaded Amestris, who already suspected, and would now, he feared, detect his love. So he offered her cities instead, and an army which would obey no other leader. (The last of these is a thoroughly Persian gift.) But, as nothing could prevail on Artaynte to change her mind, at the last he gave her the robe. Then Artaynte was very greatly rejoiced, and often wore the garment and was proud of it.

In the years after his defeat in Greece, Xerxes' empire began to wither away at its borders, as neighboring countries began to revolt after seeing Persia weak and lacking in military power. Xerxes, however, never strayed far from his seat of luxury in one of his palaces *(above in ruins)*, and was more concerned with his love affairs than his affairs of state.

And so it came to the ears of Amestris that the robe had been given to her.

Surprisingly, Queen Amestris was not angry with Artaynte. Instead she blamed Artaynte's mother, the wife of Masistes, and decided that she needed to die for her actions.

She waited, therefore, till her husband gave the great royal banquet, a feast which takes place once every year, in celebration of the king's birthday . . . this is the only day in all the year on which the king soaps his head, and distributes gifts to the Persians. Amestris waited, accordingly, for this day, and then made request of Xerxes, that he would please give to her, as her present, the wife of Masistes.

At first, Xerxes refused his wife's request. Worn down by her demands, however—and constrained by the fact that no one who asked for a gift on the king's birthday could be denied—he gave her what she wanted. Herodotus described the results:

Amestris sent for the spearmen of the royal body-guard, and caused the wife of Masistes to be mutilated in a horrible fashion. Her two breasts, her nose, ears, and lips were cut off and thrown to the dogs; her tongue was torn out by the roots, and thus disfigured she was sent back to her home.

Masistes, who knew nothing of what had happened, but fearful that some calamity had befallen him, ran hastily to his house. There, finding his wife so savagely used, he forthwith took counsel with his sons, and, accompanied by them and certain others also, set forth on way to Bactria, intending to stir up revolt in that province, and hoping to do great hurt to Xerxes: all which, I believe, he would have accomplished, if he had once reached the Bactrian and Sacan people; for he was greatly beloved by them both, and was moreover satrap of Bactria. But Xerxes, hearing of his designs, sent an armed force upon his track, and slew him while he was still upon the road, with his sons and his whole army. Such is the tale of King Xerxes' love and of the death of his brother Masistes.

Unfortunately, this tale serves as a good example of Xerxes' life following his defeat in Greece. He became more and more involved in his household intrigues, settling arguments among his wives, concubines, sons, and the court eunuchs.

The eunuchs—castrated male servants—had long been used as guards and attendants for the women of the court. Deeply involved in court intrigue, the eunuchs, sharp-tongued and often spiteful, used Xerxes' wives to influence the king himself.

Living in his palaces at Susa and Persepolis, and bitter about his losses, Xerxes was fully aware that he would never again be able to raise a mighty army and march forth to conquer other nations. His beloved Immortals had, almost to a man, perished in Greece. Tens of thousands of other soldiers had died as well—it would take a generation or more to repopulate the military. With his days of conquest over, Xerxes settled into a life of ritual and luxury, even as corruption and rot spread throughout his kingdom. The American historian Will Durant described Persia in Xerxes' later days as "a corrupt and corrupting multitude of menials filled the houses of the wealthy, while drunkenness became the common vice of every class."

The historian A.T. Olmstead, in his book *History of the Persian Empire*, offers a glimpse of what Xerxes' court at this time must have looked like. He described a king with bulging eyes, a slightly curved nose with a firm mouth, and a drooping mustache. His beard was cut square, imitating the Assyrian style with its rows of horizontal curls.

His outer robe, called the *candys,* was dyed purple and embroidered with fighting hawks or monsters. The robe was worn over the purple chiton with white spots, which was reserved for the king alone. His trousers were white or crimson, fringed with purple. His pointed shoes were blue or saffron. He was adorned with gold bracelets and a gold collar, and a golden girdle supported his sword, whose sheath was reported to be a single precious stone. In his right hand he carried a gold scepter; in his left hand he held a lotus with two buds.

Xerxes was accompanied by two attendants, who also wore robes and purple shoes. Their hats, however, sat lower, and their beards were rounded instead of square. One held over Xerxes' head a royal parasol, which always accompanied the king. The other, the chamberlain, held the royal flyswatter.

The king took his seat under a canopy, which was encrusted with jewels and supported by golden pillars. Rosettes bordered two bands, where the royal symbol was saluted by roaring lions. The throne was wood plated with gold; the feet were lion's paws that rested on balls of silver. The king's feet rested on a footstool ending in the hoofs of bulls.

When the king entered the room, all present had to prostrate themselves in adoration. Hands were kept within sleeves to prevent the possibility of assassination. The throne could be inspected on the king's departure, but it would mean death to sit upon it or even to walk on the king's rug. Xerxes was, in every sense, treated like a god.

THE GREEKS RETURN

The Greek problem never ended for Xerxes. He learned that the Athenians, under the command of Xanthippus, had captured the Persian fortress of Sestos on the Hellespont. Ruled by Artacytes, one of the king's satraps—"a Persian, but a wicked and cruel man"—the fortress had been under siege by the Athenians when they were joined by the Greeks who lived on the coast of Asia Minor, themselves subjects of the Persian Empire. Xerxes was beginning to lose control of the nations on the edge of his empire.

News also came from Greece that Themistocles, the man who had saved Athens, had been banished from that very city. Sometime between 476 and 471 B.C., accused of bribery and arrogance, he traveled from Athens to Argos. There, the Spartans further accused him of plotting with Persia, and he fled to Corcyra, then to Admetus, king of Molossia, and finally to Asia Minor. He was proclaimed a traitor by Athens, and his property was confiscated.

Themistocles made an appearance at the Xerxes' palace, where he cleverly claimed for himself the reward that was being offered for his capture. It is unclear whether he appeared before Xerxes or his son Artaxerxes; whatever the case, the Persians were impressed by his bravery. Xerxes, the man who was capable of such cruelty, took this opportunity to demonstrate his generous side. Instead of having Themistocles killed, he offered him refuge instead.

Themistocles settled in Magnesia, on the Maeander River. The revenues of this town were assigned to him for his bread, those of Myus for his condiments, and those of Lampsacus for his wine. He died at Magnesia, possibly due to illness, although the Greek historian Thucydides claims that he may have taken poison because he was unable to keep the promises he had made to Xerxes.

THE DEATH OF XERXES

Xerxes had three sons who were best placed to succeed him on the throne: each of them had royal blood from both his mother and father. The eldest of the three was Darius, named after Xerxes' father. The second was Hystaspes, and Artaxerxes was the youngest.

Hystaspes had been appointed satrap in Bactria, in the northeastern region of the empire. The other two sons remained at court, according to the fifth-century Greek historian Ctesias. Each of the three was certain that he should succeed his father on the throne, and each plotted and maneuvered to make certain that it would be so.

Artabanos, a vizier, became a key figure in the continuous round of plots and counterplots. Artabanos despised Xerxes, blaming him for the defeat in Greece and the shame brought upon the empire.

His coconspirator was the eunuch who attended Xerxes, Aspamitres. He was also aided by the general Megabyzus, the king's own son-in-law, who was angry that Xerxes had refused to take action on the charge that his wife, Amytis, was an adulteress.

Ultimately, Xerxes had made too many enemies during his reign. Late one August night in 465 B.C., Xerxes was murdered in his bedchamber.

The Tomb of Xerxes *(above)* is unmarked and cut into a stone cliff. Despite allowing his empire to decay at the end of his life, Xerxes was appreciated for some of his contributions to the monarchy. Assassinated by one son and succeeded by another, Xerxes still maintained enough respect with his subjects that a year of mourning was declared after his death.

By tradition, his successor should have been his eldest son Darius. Darius, though, seemed a logical suspect in his father's murder, since his wife had fallen in love with Xerxes. As a result, it was relatively simple for Artabanos to persuade the 18-year-old Artaxerxes to murder his older brother Darius as revenge for his father's death. Artaxerxes then claimed the throne for himself.

Artabanos soon had a falling out with the new king and tried to have him killed, hoping to claim the throne for himself. His coconspirator Megabyzus helped to betray the assassination, and Artaxerxes was only wounded in the attempt. Artabanos lost his life in the ensuing struggle.

The wily eunuch Aspamitres was put to death by a particularly inhuman type of punishment called "the boat." Plutarch described it in his book *Artaxerxes* as follows:

> Two boats being built of the same size and shape, in the one they lay the man destined for the torture, and putting the other atop of him, join the two together in such a way that his hands and feet are left outside, while the whole of the rest of his body (except the head) is imprisoned. They supply the man with food, and by prodding his eyes with sharp points force him to eat even against his will. But on his eating, they pour by way of drink into his mouth a mixture of milk and honey, and smear his face with the same. Also turning about the boat they so arrange it that his eyes are always facing the sun, and his head and face are covered every day with a host of flies that settle upon them. Moreover as he does inside the closed boats those things which men are bound of necessity to do after eating and drinking, the resulting corruption and putrefaction give birth to swarms of worms of diverse sorts, which penetrating inside his clothes, eat away his flesh. For when, after the man is dead, the upper boat is removed, his body is seen to be all gnawed away, and all about his innards is found a multitude of these and the like insects. . . .

It is written that it could take as long as 18 days for the prisoner to die.

The three surviving sons of Artabanos perished in a later battle, and Megabyzus was seriously wounded. Xerxes' second son, Hystaspes, still satrap at Bactria, revolted. The first battle was a draw, but in the second, Artaxerxes, aided by a strong wind blowing directly into his enemies' faces, achieved victory.

Alexander the Great Conquers Persia

In 334 B.C., Alexander the Great, king of Macedonia, led his Greek and Macedonian army across the Hellespont into Persia, following the same path in reverse that Xerxes had taken during his invasion of Greece.

Instead of crossing the Hellespont on a bridge of boats, Alexander moved his smaller, more mobile army across in a fleet of merchant ships. Like Xerxes, Alexander visited the ancient city of Troy, laying flowers at the graves of Achilles and Patroclus.

The Battle of the Granicus River was his first victory in a series of battles across the empire, as Alexander slowly chipped away at the rule of then king Darius III. After defeating Darius at the Battle of Issus, near the northeasternmost shore of the Mediterranean, Alexander turned his attention away from Persia itself and moved to conquer Tyre, Egypt, and Syria.

The Battle of Gaugamela (on October 1 in 331 B.C.) was the last major stand of the Persian army. Alexander moved through Babylon and then captured the four Persian capitals of Susa, Persepolis, Parsagard, and Ecbatana. When Darius III was killed by his cousin Bessus in the spring of 330 B.C., the Persian Empire came to an end. Once the greatest empire the world had ever seen, it had been defeated by the very people Xerxes had set out to conquer just 150 years earlier.

Artaxerxes ruled for 40 years over the slowly declining Persian Empire. He even signed a formal peace treaty with Athens in 449 B.C. He was known for his gentle and compassionate nature, so unlike the Persian kings who had preceded him.

As king and royal son, one of his first acts was to order Xerxes' funeral. Representatives were sent from each part of the kingdom to honor the king, and a one-year mourning period was declared. Xerxes was buried in a rock-cut tomb he had excavated in the cliff to the east of his father's. No inscription was made on the tomb.

WHO WAS XERXES?

Historians are divided in their assessments of Xerxes. Peter Green says, "His record contains a long list of military successes . . . Xerxes was a remarkable religious reformer, and a scarcely less remarkable patron of the arts." In contrast, C. Hignett, a British historian, says, "He was not equal to his high position, which he owed to his birth and not his merits . . . he was lecherous and cruel."

The record shows that both views are correct. Like most leaders, Xerxes was a combination of good and bad. He was born to greatness. Even the Greek Herodotus said, "Among all this multitude of men there was not one who, for beauty and stature, deserved more than Xerxes himself to wield so vast a power."

Like many men who "wield so vast a power," Xerxes made mistakes. He felt that he was invincible, yet he was defeated by a much smaller force. He could be almost inconceivably cruel, yet he left behind cities like Persepolis that give witness to his glory and greatness. It is because of this very combination of greatness and failure that Xerxes has continued to be an object of fascination for nearly 2,500 years.

CHRONOLOGY

◆ ◆ ◆

521 B.C.   Darius I becomes ruler of Persia; his empire consists of more than 20 provinces, including Egypt and Babylon; encompassing approximately 7.5 million square kilometers, it is territorially the largest empire of classical antiquity.

ca. 519   Xerxes is born.

492   The Persian Wars begin.

490   The Persians are defeated by the Athenians at the Battle of Marathon.

486   Upon the death of Darius I, Xerxes assumes the throne of Persia.

486–481   Xerxes leads an expedition to Egypt and squashes the rebellion.

482   Xerxes puts down the rebellion in Babylon.

480   Xerxes invades Greece; he defeats the Spartans at the Battle of Thermopylae; the Persian fleet loses to the Greeks at Salamis; and Xerxes is forced to retreat with the majority of the army back to Persia.

479   The remaining Persian forces in Greece are defeated.

465   Xerxes is assassinated; his son Artaxerxes becomes king of Persia.

BIBLIOGRAPHY

◆ ◆ ◆

Abbot, Jacob. *History of Xerxes the Great*. Philadelphia: Henry Altemus Company, 1900.

Crompton, Samuel Willard. *Alexander the Great*. New York: Chelsea House Publishers, 2003.

Golding, William. *The Hot Gates and Other Occasional Pieces*. New York: Harcourt Brace Jovanovich, 1965.

Green, Peter. *The Greco-Persian Wars*. Berkeley: University of California Press, 1996.

Herodotus. *The Histories*. New York: Alfred A. Knopf, 1997.

Hornblower, Simon, and Antony Spawforth. *The Oxford Companion to Classical Civilization*. Oxford, UK: Oxford University Press, 1998.

Horne, Charles F., ed. "The Kurash Prism," Iran Chamber Society. Available online. www.iranchamber.com/history/cyrus/cyrus_decree_jews.php.

Llywelyn, Morgan. *Xerxes*. New York: Chelsea House Publishers, 1987.

Olmstead, A.T. *History of the Persian Empire*. Chicago: The University of Chicago Press, 1948.

Wilber, Donald N. *Persepolis: The Archaeology of Parsa, Seat of the Persian Kings*. New York: Thomas Y. Crowell Company, 1969.

FURTHER READING

◆ ◆ ◆

Herodotus. *The Histories*. New York: Alfred A. Knopf, 1997.

Miller, Frank. *300*. Milwaukie, OR: Dark Horse, 1999.

Nelson, Richard. *Armies of the Greek and Persian Wars: 500 to 350 B.C.* Goring-by-Sea, U.K.: War Games Research Group, 1975.

Pressfield, Steven. *Gates of Fire: An Epic Novel of the Battle of Thermopylae*. New York: Bantam, 1999.

Sam, Amini. *Pictorial History of Ancient Persia*. Bloomington, Ind.: Authorhouse, 2006.

Souza, Philip. *The Greek and Persian Wars 499–386 B.C.* Oxford, UK: Osprey Publishing, 2003.

Strauss, Barry. *The Battle of Salamis: The Naval Encounter that Saved Greece—and Western Civilization*. New York: Simon & Schuster, 2004.

Xenophon. *The Persian Expedition*. New York: Penguin, 1950.

WEB SITES

Iran Chamber Society
www.iranchamber.com

Military History
http://militaryhistory.about.com/od/grecopersianwars/The_Greek_and_Persian_Wars_490479_BC.htm

PHOTO CREDITS

◆ ◆ ◆

INDEX

◆◆◆

ABOUT THE AUTHORS

◆ ◆ ◆

DENNIS ABRAMS is the author of numerous books for Chelsea House, including biographies of Barbara Park, Ty Cobb, Hamid Karzai, Eminem, and Thabo Mbeki. He attended Antioch College, where he majored in English and communications. Abrams currently resides in Houston, Texas, with his partner of 18 years.

ARTHUR M. SCHLESINGER, JR. was the leading American historian of our time. He won the Pulitzer Prize for his books *The Age of Jackson* (1945) and *A Thousand Days* (1965), which also won the National Book Award. Professor Schlesinger was the Albert Schweitzer Professor of the Humanities at the City University of New York and was involved in several other Chelsea House projects, including the series *Revolutionary War Leaders*, *Colonial Leaders*, and *Your Government*.